Publishing

SAS® Statistics by Example

Ron Cody

THE
POWER
TO KNOW.

33.55

The correct bibliographic citation for this manual is as follows: Cody, Ron. 2011. *SAS® Statistics by Example.* Cary, NC: SAS Institute Inc.

SAS® Statistics by Example

Copyright © 2011, SAS Institute Inc., Cary, NC, USA

ISBN 978-1-61290-012-4 (electronic book)
ISBN 978-1-60764-800-0

All rights reserved. Produced in the United States of America.

SAS Institute Inc., SAS Campus Drive, Cary, North Carolina 27513-2414

1st printing, August 2011

SAS® Publishing provides a complete selection of books and electronic products to help customers use SAS software to its fullest potential. For more information about our e-books, e-learning products, CDs, and hard-copy books, visit the SAS Publishing Web site at **support.sas.com/publishing** or call 1-800-727-3228.

SAS® and all other SAS Institute Inc. product or service names are registered trademarks or trademarks of SAS Institute Inc. in the USA and other countries. ® indicates USA registration.

Other brand and product names are registered trademarks or trademarks of their respective companies.

Contents

List of Programs

Chapter 4

Chapter 5

Chapter 6

Chapter 13

Chapter 14

Acknowledgments

A tremendous amount of work went into bringing this book to the bookshelf, and all that work wasn't done by me alone. Several factors combined to make the review process and the final production of this book a challenge.

First and foremost, I would like to thank John West, my editor and friend, who was amazingly patient and calm, even when there were technical challenges to overcome.

Next, we enlisted the help of more reviewers than usual. Four of these reviewers read the book from cover to cover and made excellent suggestions for improvements and found some subtle and obscure errors. So, kudos to Gerry Hobbs, Catherine Truxillo, Jeff Smith, and Marc Huber.

Other reviewers read chapters, particularly those where they had a particular expertise. Sincere thanks to Rob Agnelli, Paul Grant, Sanjay Matange, David Schlotzhauer, Jim Seabolt, and Sue Walsh.

Since the decision was made to use HTML output instead of simple list output, considerable extra effort was required. The production team needed to "touch" approximately 161 image files so that they would look good both in print as well as on the various eBook devices. The people involved in this process were: Jennifer Dilley, designer; Candy Farrell, technical publishing specialist; Joan Celmer, copyeditor; and Mary Beth Steinbach, managing editor.

No book would be successful without having people to market it. Thanks to Aimee Rodriguez and Stacey Hamilton for this essential task.

Finally, I salute the artists who created the front and back covers of the book. Nice job Jennifer Dilley and Marchellina Waugh.

Ron Cody, Summer 2011

An Introduction to SAS

Introduction

If you are reading this book, you are probably familiar with various statistical techniques but might not have used SAS to analyze data. The primary purpose of this book is to show you how to use SAS to perform a variety of statistical tasks. To that end, this book provides examples of many of the commonly used statistical techniques. Following each example is a discussion of the output. Although this is not a book about SAS programming, many of the examples require some data manipulation tasks, which will be described. If you need to gain more SAS programming skills, see *Learning SAS by Example: A Programmer's Guide*, also by this author and published by SAS Press.

This book is divided into five sections: An Introduction to SAS, Descriptive Statistics, Inferential Statistics, Power/Sample size calculations, and Selecting Random Samples.

All of the programs and data files in this book are available from SAS Press. To download these programs and files, go to http://support.sas.com/authors.

If you already have some familiarity with SAS data sets and how to run SAS programs, you can skip this chapter and start right in with Chapter 2.

The remainder of this chapter describes what SAS is, the basic structure of SAS programs, how to access some simple data sets, and how to run a SAS program on a Windows platform.

What is SAS

SAS (pronounced sass) is a collection of programs that are used to read data from a variety of sources (text files, Excel workbooks, various databases, etc.), to manipulate data with a very powerful programming language, and to perform various reporting and data analysis tasks. To run all of the examples in this book, you will need access to Base SAS, SAS/STAT, and SAS/GRAPH software.

SAS runs on many different computing platforms: PCs, UNIX and Linux operating systems, and mainframe computers. You can run the examples in this book on any of these platforms, although there are some small differences in how the data are accessed on the various systems. The examples in this book were all run on a PC, because this is by far the most popular platform on which SAS is run.

Statistical Tasks Performed by SAS

SAS, like many other statistical packages, has built-in procedures for analyzing data. These procedures (called PROCs for short) enable you to perform statistical tests and analyses. For example, if you want to perform a Student's *t*-test, you use PROC TTEST, to run a regression model, you use PROC REG. The list of statistical PROCs is quite extensive, and not all of them are covered in this book. Even so, this book is a good place to get started, and many of the most popular statistical tasks are covered. The complete guide to all SAS/STAT procedures is available from SAS Institute. The documentation is available in more than five volumes (taking up about two feet of shelf space) or for free in HTML or PDF form on the SAS Web site: http://support.sas.com/documentation. Select SAS Press books are also available on iPad, Kindle, Google eBooks, Mobipocket, Books24x7, netLibrary, and Safari Books online.

The Structure of SAS Programs

SAS programs are divided into DATA and PROC steps. With DATA steps you can read text data from files; create new variables from existing variables; perform logical operations on your data; and merge, concatenate, and subset your data files. PROC steps give you the ability to perform pre-defined tasks such as creating frequency distributions or performing a *t*-test. SAS stores data in data sets that are unique to SAS. Your data might already be in a SAS data set, in which case you might not need to write a DATA step at all. However, even if you are starting with data already in a SAS data set, you might want to write a DATA step to perform some manipulation of the data, such as performing a transformation, grouping values, subsetting your data, or combining data from several data sets.

SAS Data Sets

SAS data sets consist of two parts: a descriptor portion, or *metadata* (information about your data set, such as the variable names and data types), and the data values themselves. SAS can create SAS data sets from almost any source. If you have raw data in a text file, you can use a DATA step to read the file and create your SAS data set. If you have an Excel workbook, or any one of several popular database formats, you can either use a SAS procedure to convert the data into a SAS data set or use the Import Wizard (part of SAS/ACCESS and available from SAS Institute) to point-and-click your way through the conversion.

SAS Display Manager

This section shows you how to run SAS programs on a Windows platform. If you are using UNIX or a mainframe to run your programs, your screens will not look like the images shown in this section. If you choose to use SAS Enterprise Guide to run your SAS programs on a Windows platform, you will also be using a different editor.

When you open SAS on a PC platform, you enter SAS Display Manager. This facility contains three major windows: the Program Editor, where you write, edit, and submit your SAS programs; a Log window, where you see error messages and information about the program you have submitted; and the Output window, where SAS displays your output. If you need the output for a Web page or you want to use the output in a Word or Word Perfect program, the Output Delivery System (ODS) can send your output to these destinations as HTML, RTF (rich text format), or PDF.

The following display shows SAS Display Manager with all three windows open:

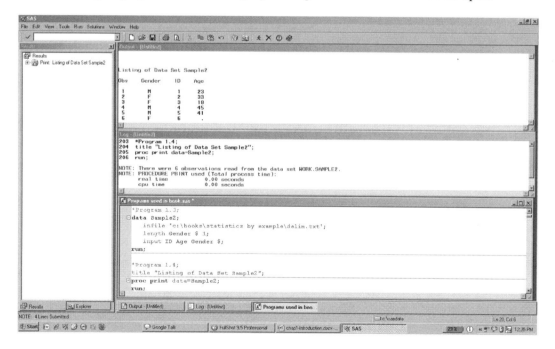

The top section is the Output window, the middle section is the Log window, and the bottom section is the Program Editor window. You can resize, move, or expand each of these windows.

Excel Workbooks

Because Excel workbooks (or comma-separated values [CSV] files) are so popular on PCs, let's examine how to use the SAS Import Wizard to convert these files into SAS data sets.

The following display shows an Excel workbook called SAMPLE.XLS:

Each of the columns in this workbook contains information about each of our subjects (ID, Age, and Gender). The first row of the workbook contains variable names. In Excel, these names can be anything. In SAS, variable names must conform to a stricter naming convention. The maximum length of a SAS variable name is 32 characters; the first character of a variable name must be a letter or an underscore, and the remaining characters of the variable name can contain letters (uppercase or lowercase), numbers, and the underscore character. For example, Age, Income2010, and Home_Runs are valid SAS variable names; 1year, Year Income, and Cost% are not valid SAS variable names. Later you will see what happens if the first row of your workbook contains variable names that are not valid SAS variable names.

By the way, SAS variable names are not case sensitive. However, if you use uppercase, lowercase, or mixed case, SAS remembers the case of the variable name from the first time you used it and displays the names in SAS reports based on the previous value.

Each of the rows of the workbook, with the exception of the first row, contains data about an individual. SAS calls these rows *observations*. So, whereas an Excel workbook has columns and rows, SAS data sets have *variables* and *observations*.

To convert this Excel file into a SAS data set, you can use the Import Wizard:

1. Click File.

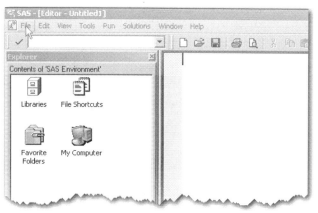

2. Select Import Data.

3. Choose Microsoft Excel.

4. Select the Excel workbook that you want to convert.

5. Name the SAS data set (SampleData in this example).

6. Click Finish (at the bottom right of the window) to complete the conversion.

Naming conventions for SAS data sets are the same as for SAS variable names. The names must be 32 characters or less in length, they must start with a letter or an underscore, and the remaining characters must be letters, numbers, or underscores.

Now that you have converted your Excel workbook into a temporary SAS data set, you can list the observations in the data set and inspect the descriptor portion of the data set. SAS provides you with several ways to do this.

One way to see a listing of the data in a SAS data set is to use a SAS procedure called PROC PRINT. The following program demonstrates how to use PROC PRINT to list the observations in the SampleData data set:

Program 1.1: Using PROC PRINT to List the Observations in a SAS Data Set

```
proc print data=SampleData;
run;
```

Amazingly enough, this is a complete SAS program. Notice that each statement in this two-line SAS program ends in a semicolon. When you write SAS programs, you can use as many lines as you want to write a statement; you can even put more than one statement on a line (though this is not recommended for stylistic reasons). The semicolon is the logical end of a SAS statement. You are free to add extra spaces on a line or place extra blank lines in your program to make it more readable.

To run this program from Display Manager, click the **Submit** icon:

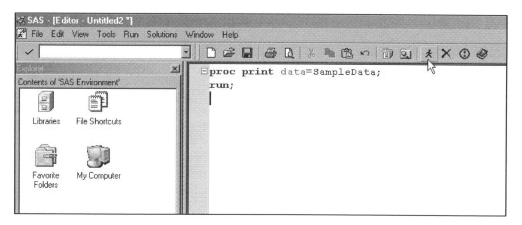

Here is the output you get from running Program 1.1:

Obs	ID	Age	Gender
1	1	23	M
2	2	33	F
3	3	18	F
4	4	45	M
5	5	41	M

At the top of the three right-most columns, you see the SAS variable names—the same names that were stored in the first row of your workbook. The first column, labeled Obs (short for Observations), was generated by SAS and shows the observation number.

Each row of the listing represents a row from the workbook.

Next, let's see how to display the data descriptor portion of this data set. Program 1.2 is one way to do this:

Program 1.2: Using PROC CONTENTS to Display the Data Descriptor Portion of a SAS Data Set

```
title "Displaying the Descriptor Portion of a SAS Data Set";
proc contents data=SampleData;
run;
```

Notice that I have added a TITLE statement to this program. With a TITLE statement, you can enter a title that will print across the top of every page of output. TITLE statements are in a class of SAS statements known as GLOBAL statements. The title that you enter stays in effect for the remainder of your SAS session, unless you replace it with another TITLE statement. To remove all titles from your output, submit a null title statement like this:

```
title;
```

When you submit Program 1.2, you will see the following output:

Displaying the Descriptor Portion of a SAS Data Set

The CONTENTS Procedure

Data Set Name	WORK.SAMPLEDATA	Observations	5
Member Type	DATA	Variables	3
Engine	V9	Indexes	0
Created	Friday, May 06, 2011 02:31:59 PM	Observation Length	24
Last Modified	Friday, May 06, 2011 02:31:59 PM	Deleted Observations	0
Protection		Compressed	NO
Data Set Type		Sorted	NO
Label			
Data Representation	WINDOWS_32		
Encoding	wlatin1 Western (Windows)		

Engine/Host Dependent Information	
Data Set Page Size	4096
Number of Data Set Pages	1
First Data Page	1
Max Obs per Page	168
Obs in First Data Page	5
Number of Data Set Repairs	0
Filename	C:\DOCUME~1\Ron\LOCALS~1\Temp\SAS Temporary Files_TD4228\sampledata.sas7bdat
Release Created	9.0201M0
Host Created	XP_PRO

Alphabetic List of Variables and Attributes					
#	Variable	Type	Len	Format	Informat	Label
2	Age	Num	8			Age
3	Gender	Char	1	$1.	$1.	Gender
1	ID	Num	8			ID

The first two lines of output show that the data set name is SAMPLEDATA. (The full name is WORK.SAMPLEDATA. The prefix WORK. tells SAS that this is a temporary SAS data set.) Also shown in these lines are the number of observations (5) and the number of variables (3). Let's skip down to the portion of the output labeled Alphabetic List of Variables and Attributes. Here you see that the variables Age and ID are stored as numeric types and Gender is stored as a character type.

Variable Types in SAS Data Sets

SAS has only two variable types: numeric and character. By default, all numeric values are stored in 8 bytes, allowing for approximately 15 significant figures, depending on your operating system. Character values are stored 1 byte per character and can be from 1 to 32,767 bytes in length.

Temporary versus Permanent SAS Data Sets

SAS data sets can be either temporary or permanent. A temporary SAS data set is one that exists for the duration of your SAS session but is not saved when you exit SAS. Permanent SAS data sets, as the name implies, remain when you exit SAS and can be accessed in future SAS sessions. The Import Wizard example discussed previously used the Work library. Choosing the Work library caused the SAS data set SAMPLEDATA to be a temporary data set.

SAS data set identifiers are divided into two parts, separated by a period. The part before the period is called a library reference (libref for short) and identifies the folder where SAS has stored the data set. The part following the period is the data set name. Both parts of this identifier must satisfy the naming conventions mentioned earlier.

For example, if your data set is called SURVEY and is stored in a library called MYDATA, SAS uses the following notation to identify the file:

```
mydata.survey
```

If you wanted to put this file on your disk drive in the **C:\MYSASFILES** folder, you would write a statement called a LIBNAME statement that associates the **c:\sasfiles** folder with the MYDATA library reference, like this:

```
libname mydata 'c:\mysasfiles';
```

Creating a SAS Data Set from Raw Data

If you have your data in a text file, SAS can read the text file and create a SAS data set. The text file can contain either data values separated by delimiters or data values in fixed columns.

Data Values Separated by Delimiters

SAS can read data values from a text file in which each value is separated from the next value by a delimiter. By default, SAS expects one or more spaces between data values. However, it is easy to specify other delimiters, such as commas. Let's start by reading a small text file in which spaces are used as delimiters. Here's a listing of this file:

Raw Data with Blanks as Delimiters: File c:\books\Statistics by Example\delim.txt

```
1 23 M
2 33 F
3  18    F
4 45    M
5 41 M
6 . F
```

In this file, the three data values on each line represent an ID number, Age, and Gender, respectively. Before you write a SAS program to read this text file, notice that ID = 6 has a missing value for her age. Because you have delimited data, you need a way to specify that the Age value is missing for that subject. When you have blanks as delimiters, you can use a period to specify that you have a missing value. In the next example, which uses a CSV file, you do not need to use periods for missing values.

Program 1.3 will read this text file and create a SAS data set called Sample2:

Program 1.3: Reading Data from a Text File That Uses Spaces as Delimiters

```
data Sample2;
    infile 'c:\books\statistics by example\delim.txt';
    length Gender $ 1;
    input ID Age Gender $;
run;
```

The INFILE statement tells SAS where to look for the text file. Following the keyword INFILE, you place the filename in single or double quotes. The LENGTH statement tells SAS that the variable Gender is character (the dollar sign indicates this) and that you want to store Gender in 1 byte (the 1 indicates this). The INPUT statement lists the variable names in the same order as the values in the text file. Because you already told SAS that Gender is a character variable, the dollar sign following the name Gender on the INPUT statement is not necessary. If you had not included a LENGTH statement, the dollar sign following Gender on the INPUT statement would have been necessary. SAS assumes variables are numeric unless you tell it otherwise.

The RUN statement ends the program. Because this program starts with the keyword DATA, it is called a DATA step. The previous two programs demonstrated PROC steps. SAS programs are typically made up of DATA and PROC steps. Each step ends with a RUN statement.

As you did earlier, you can use PROC PRINT to list the observations in the Sample2 data set (as shown in Program 1.4):

Program 1.4: Using PROC PRINT to List the Observations in Data Set Sample2

```
title "Listing of Data Set Sample2";
proc print data=Sample2;
run;
```

Here is the listing:

Listing of Data Set Sample2

Obs	Gender	ID	Age
1	M	1	23
2	F	2	33
3	F	3	18
4	M	4	45
5	M	5	41
6	F	6	.

Reading CSV Files

You can make a very small change to Program 1.3 to read the same data from a CSV file. Following is a listing of such a file:

A CSV Text File: c:\books\Statistics by Example\comma.csv

```
1,23,M
2,33,F
3,18,F
4,45,M
5,41,M
6,,F
```

Notice that you no longer need the period in subject 6 because, in the tradition of CSV files, two commas in a row indicate a missing value.

The only change you need to make to Program 1.3 is to use an option called DSD on the INFILE statement. The DSD option specifies that two consecutive commas represent a missing value and that the default delimiter is a comma. Here is the modified program:

Program 1.5: Reading a CSV File

```
data Sample2;
   infile 'c:\books\statistics by example\comma.csv' dsd;
   length Gender $ 1;
   input ID Age Gender $;
run;
```

This program produces a SAS data set identical to the one created by Program 1.3.

If your CSV file contains variable names in the first row, then the Import Wizard uses these variable names when it creates the SAS data set. Actually, you can use the Import Wizard even if the first row does not contain variable names. If you do, SAS will name the variables F1, F2, etc. This approach is not recommended.

Data Values in Fixed Columns

You might have a raw text file in which the value for each variable is in a fixed column. SAS has two methods for reading this type of data: column input and formatted input. For column input, you follow each variable name on the INPUT statement with the starting and ending column for that value. If you want to create a character variable, you place a dollar sign between the variable name and the column specifications.

For example, if you have ID data in columns 1–3, Age in columns 4–6, and Gender in column 7 of your raw data file, your input statement might look like this:

```
input ID $ 1-3 Age 4-6 Gender $ 7;
```

Stylistically, you might prefer to write this statement on three lines, like this (so that the variable names line up):

```
input ID     $ 1-3
      Age       4-6
      Gender $ 7;
```

For formatted input, you specify the starting column for the variable using an at sign (@) (called a *column pointer*) followed by the starting column number. Next, you put your variable name, followed by a *SAS informat*—a specification of how to read and interpret the next *n* columns. An equivalent statement to read the same data for ID, Age, and Gender using formatted input is:

```
input @1 ID     $3.
      @4 Age      3.
      @7 Gender $1.;
```

The informat $3. tells SAS to read three columns of character data; the 3. informat says to read three columns of numeric data; the $1. informat says to read one column of character data. The two informats *n*. and $*n*., are used to read *n* columns of numeric and character data, respectively.

The INPUT statement is actually quite powerful and enables you to read both simple and complex data structures. For a complete description of how the INPUT statement works, see *Learning SAS by Example: A Programmer's Guide* or one of the other publications available from SAS Press.

Excel Files with Invalid SAS Variable Names

What if your Excel file contains variable names in the first row that are not valid SAS names? Take a look at the following spreadsheet:

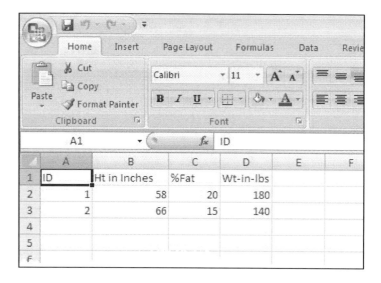

Three of the four variable names are not valid SAS variable names because they contain either blanks or invalid characters (percent sign and dashes). What happens when you use the Import Wizard to convert this spreadsheet into a SAS data set? SAS substitutes an underscore character in place of each invalid character in the name. A SAS data set created from this spreadsheet would contain the variables ID, Ht_in_Inches, _Fat, and Wt_in_Lbs.

It is possible to use SAS variable names that contain invalid characters. To include such variables, you need to set a system option called VALIDVARNAMES and refer to the variable names using a special notation. Using such variables is not recommended, however, because doing so creates added complications.

Other Sources of Data

The bottom line is that SAS can read data from just about anywhere. Using the Import Wizard, for example, you can read Excel, Access, CSV, tab-delimited, dBASE, JMP (a SAS product), Lotus, SPSS, Stata, and Paradox files. In addition, SAS can read data from most of the major mainframe database systems such as Oracle and DB2.

Conclusions

You now know how to use the Display Manager or other editor to write your SAS programs, and you know how to read your data from a variety of sources. Now you are ready to start using SAS procedures to analyze your data. In the remaining chapters of this book, you will learn how to create descriptive statistics and how to run most of the commonly used inferential statistical tasks.

Descriptive Statistics – Continuous Variables

Introduction

One of the first steps in any statistical analysis is to calculate some basic descriptive statistics on the variables of interest. SAS has a number of procedures that provide tabular as well as graphical displays of your data.

To demonstrate some of the ways that SAS can produce descriptive statistics, use a data set called `Blood_Pressure`. This data set contains the variables Subj (ID value for each subject), Drug (with values of `Placebo`, `Drug A`, or `Drug B`), SBP (systolic blood pressure), DBP (diastolic blood pressure), and Gender (with values of M or F). Here is a listing of the first 25 observations from this data set:

First 25 Observations from Blood_Pressure

Drug	Subj	Gender	SBP	DBP
Placebo	1	M	138	86
Placebo	2	F	124	82
Placebo	3	M	150	72
Placebo	4		136	84
Placebo	5	M	.	.
Placebo	6	F	132	84
Placebo	7	M	130	84
Placebo	8	F	146	88
Placebo	9	M	134	82
Placebo	10	F	138	88
Placebo	11	M	144	84
Placebo	12	F	130	88
Placebo	13	M	134	80
Placebo	14	F	132	90
Placebo	15	M	.	.
Placebo	16	F	124	88
Placebo	17	M	140	78
Placebo	18		156	86
Placebo	19	M	120	80
Placebo	20	F	142	90
Drug A	21	M	126	76
Drug A	22	F	134	86
Drug A	23	M	118	78
Drug A	24	F	132	80
Drug A	25	M	.	.

Notice that some of the observations contain missing values, represented by periods for numeric values and blanks for character values

---

Computing Descriptive Statistics Using PROC MEANS

One way to compute means and standard deviations is to use PROC MEANS. Here is a program to compute some basic descriptive statistics on the two variables SBP and DBP:

Program 2.1: **Generating Descriptive Statistics with PROC MEANS**

```
libname example 'c:\books\statistics by example';

title "Descriptive Statistics for SBP and DBP";
proc means data=example.Blood_Pressure n nmiss mean std median
          maxdec=3;
   var SBP DBP;
run;
```

Because the `Blood_Pressure` data set is a permanent SAS data set (when it was created, it was placed in a folder on a disk drive instead of in a temporary SAS folder that disappears when you end your SAS session), you need a LIBNAME statement to tell SAS where to find the data set. In this example, the data set is located in the **c:\books\statistics by example** folder. Remember that SAS data set names contain two parts: the part before the period is a library reference (libref for short) that tells SAS where to find the data set, and the part after the period is the actual data set name (in this case, `Blood_Pressure`). If you were to use your operating system to list the contents of the **c:\books\statistics by example** folder, you would see a file called:

```
Blood_Pressure.sas7bdat
```

This file is the actual SAS data set and contains both the descriptor portion and the individual observations. The extension sas7bdat indicates that the data set is compatible with SAS 7 and later. This file is not a text file, and you cannot view it using a word processor or other Windows programs.

The TITLE statement causes SAS to print the title at the top of every page of output until you change the title or turn off all titles. In this program, the title is placed in double quotes. You can also use single quotation marks (as long as there are no single quotation marks in the title) or, for that matter, no quotation marks at all (SAS is smart enough to realize that the text following a TITLE statement is the title text).

PROC MEANS is a popular SAS procedure that produces a number of useful statistics. In this program, the keyword DATA= tells the procedure that you want to produce descriptive statistics on the `Blood_Pressure` data set.

You can control what statistics this procedure produces by using procedure options. These options are placed between the procedure name and the semicolon ending the statement, and you can place them in any order. If you omit these options, PROC MEANS will, by default, print the number of nonmissing observations, the mean, standard deviation, the minimum value, and the maximum value.

The first two options in this program, N and NMISS, cause the number of nonmissing and missing values for each variable to be reported. The next three options, MEAN, STD, and MEDIAN, request the mean, standard deviation, and the median to be computed. The last option, MAXDEC=*n*, specifies how many digits to the right of the decimal point you want in your report. In this program, you are requesting that all the statistics be reported to three decimal places.

The following list describes some of the more useful options:

Option	Description
N	Number of nonmissing observations
NMISS	Number of observations with missing values
MEAN	Arithmetic mean
STD	Standard deviation
STDERR	Standard error
MIN	Minimum value
MAX	Maximum value
MEDIAN	Median
MAXDEC=	Maximum number of decimal places to display
CLM	95% confidence limit on the mean
CV	Coefficient of variation

The VAR statement tells the procedure which variables you want to analyze. If you omit a VAR statement, PROC MEANS produces statistics on all of the numeric variables in the specified data set (usually not a good idea).

Finally, the PROC step ends with a RUN statement. Here is the output:

Descriptive Statistics for SBP and DBP

The MEANS Procedure

Variable	N	N Miss	Mean	Std Dev	Median
SBP	56	4	130.536	10.911	132.000
DBP	56	4	81.321	5.451	82.000

Descriptive Statistics Broken Down by a Classification Variable

The data set `Blood_Pressure` also contains a variable called `Drug`. You might want to see the same statistics, but this time compute them for each level of `Drug`. One way to do this is to add a CLASS statement to PROC MEANS like this:

Program 2.2: Statistics Broken Down by a Classification Variable

```
title "Descriptive Statistics Broken Down by Drug";
proc means data=example.Blood_Pressure n nmiss mean std median
          maxdec=3;
   class Drug;
   var SBP DBP;
run;
```

The CLASS statement tells the procedure to produce the selected statistics for each unique value of **Drug**. This is a good time to tell you that when you have more than one statement in a PROC step (in this case, the CLASS and VAR statements), the order of these statements does not usually matter. The exceptions are certain statistical procedures in which you must specify your model before you ask for certain statistics.

Here is the output:

Descriptive Statistics Broken Down by Drug

The MEANS Procedure

Drug	N Obs	Variable	N	N Miss	Mean	Std Dev	Median
Drug A	20	SBP	19	1	130.211	7.941	132.000
		DBP	19	1	81.053	4.961	80.000
Drug B	20	SBP	19	1	125.579	12.712	124.000
		DBP	19	1	78.947	5.671	82.000
Placebo	20	SBP	18	2	136.111	9.317	135.000
		DBP	18	2	84.111	4.626	84.000

You should always request both the N and NMISS options when you run PROC MEANS, because missing values are a possible source of bias.

What if you want to see the grand mean, as well as the means broken down by Drug, all in one listing? The PROC MEANS option PRINTALLTYPES does this for you when you include a CLASS statement. Here is the modified program:

Program 2.3: Demonstrating the PRINTALLTYPES Option with PROC MEANS

```
title "Descriptive Statistics Broken Down by Drug";
proc means data=example.Blood_Pressure n nmiss
           mean std median  printalltypes maxdec=3;
   class Drug;
   var SBP DBP;
run;
```

Here is the corresponding output:

Descriptive Statistics Broken Down by Drug

The MEANS Procedure

N Obs	Variable	N	N Miss	Mean	Std Dev	Median
60	SBP	56	4	130.536	10.911	132.000
	DBP	56	4	81.321	5.451	82.000

Drug	N Obs	Variable	N	N Miss	Mean	Std Dev	Median
Drug A	20	SBP	19	1	130.211	7.941	132.000
		DBP	19	1	81.053	4.961	80.000
Drug B	20	SBP	19	1	125.579	12.712	124.000
		DBP	19	1	78.947	5.671	82.000
Placebo	20	SBP	18	2	136.111	9.317	135.000
		DBP	18	2	84.111	4.626	84.000

Now you see statistics for each value of Drug *and* for all subjects, in the same listing.

Computing a 95% Confidence Interval and the Standard Error

A 95% confidence interval for the mean (often abbreviated as 95% CI) is useful in helping you decide how well your sample mean estimates the mean of the population from which you took your sample. Another measure, the standard error, is also useful for the same reason. This program shows how to compute both:

Program 2.4: Computing a 95% Confidence Interval

```
title "Computing a 95% Confidence Interval and the Standard Error";
proc means data=example.Blood_Pressure n mean clm stderr
          maxdec=3;
   class Drug;
   var SBP DBP;
run;
```

In this example, some of the options that were used previously have been omitted to reduce the size of the output. This program also uses the option CLM (confidence limit for the mean) to request the interval. SAS uses this option because the upper and lower bounds on a confidence interval are also referred to as confidence limits. The option STDERR requests that the standard error also be listed in the output, which follows:

Computing a 95% Confidence Interval and the Standard Error

The MEANS Procedure

Drug	N Obs	Variable	N	Mean	Lower 95% CL for Mean	Upper 95% CL for Mean	Std Error
Drug A	20	SBP	19	130.211	126.383	134.038	1.822
		DBP	19	81.053	78.662	83.444	1.138
Drug B	20	SBP	19	125.579	119.452	131.706	2.916
		DBP	19	78.947	76.214	81.681	1.301
Placebo	20	SBP	18	136.111	131.478	140.744	2.196
		DBP	18	84.111	81.811	86.412	1.090

Producing Descriptive Statistics, Histograms, and Probability Plots

Another SAS procedure, PROC UNIVARIATE, produces output that is similar to the output from PROC MEANS. However, PROC UNIVARIATE provides additional statements that produce histograms and probability plots.

The following program demonstrates these features of PROC UNIVARIATE:

Program 2.5: Producing Histograms and Probability Plots Using PROC UNIVARIATE

```
title "Demonstrating PROC UNIVARIATE";
proc univariate data=example.Blood_Pressure;
   id Subj;
   var SBP DBP;
   histogram;
   probplot / normal(mu=est sigma=est);
run;
```

Program 2.5 demonstrates a typical use of PROC UNIVARIATE—to produce descriptive statistics and some graphical output. Note that in order to generate the histogram and probability plots, you need to have SAS/GRAPH installed.

The ID statement is not necessary, but it is particularly useful with PROC UNIVARIATE. With this statement, you can specify a variable that identifies each observation. In this example, Subj is the ID variable.

The VAR statement works with PROC UNIVARIATE in the same way that it works with PROC MEANS—it enables you to list the variables that you want to analyze.

The HISTOGRAM statement requests histograms. You can follow the HISTOGRAM statement with a list of variables. If you omit this list of variables, the procedure produces a histogram for every variable that you listed on the VAR statement.

Finally, the PROBPLOT statement requests a probability plot. This plot shows percentiles from a theoretical distribution on the x-axis and data values on the y-axis. This example program selects the normal distribution using the NORMAL option after the forward slash. If your data values are normally distributed, the points on this plot will form a straight line. To make it easier to see deviations from normality, the option NORMAL also produces a reference line where your data values would fall if they came from a normal distribution. When you use the NORMAL option, you also need to specify a mean and standard deviation. Specify these by using the keyword MU= to specify the mean and the keyword SIGMA= to specify a standard deviation. The keyword EST tells the procedure to use the data values to estimate the mean and standard deviation, instead of some theoretical value.

Notice the slash between the word PROBPLOT and NORMAL. Using a slash here follows standard SAS syntax: if you want to specify options for any statement in a PROC step, follow the statement keyword with a slash. (Note: It took the author several years to figure this out for himself.)

To save space, the following output shows only the results for the variable SBP. Each section is presented separately, with a discussion following each section.

Demonstrating PROC UNIVARIATE

The UNIVARIATE Procedure
Variable: SBP

Moments ❶			
N	56	Sum Weights	56
Mean	130.535714	Sum Observations	7310
Std Deviation	10.9111524	Variance	119.053247
Skewness	-0.1155991	Kurtosis	-0.5354758
Uncorrected SS	960764	Corrected SS	6547.92857
Coeff Variation	8.35874876	Std Error Mean	1.45806407

Basic Statistical Measures ❷			
Location		Variability	
Mean	130.5357	Std Deviation	10.91115
Median	132.0000	Variance	119.05325
Mode	134.0000	Range	48.00000
		Interquartile Range	17.00000

Tests for Location: Mu0=0 ❸				
Test		Statistic	p Value	
Student's t	t	89.52673	Pr > |t|	<.0001
Sign	M	28	Pr >= |M|	<.0001
Signed Rank	S	798	Pr >= |S|	<.0001

❶ The first section of the output contains come useful and some not-so-useful values. For example, you see the number of nonmissing values that were used to compute the statistics (N), mean, and standard deviation.

Also in this section, you see skewness and kurtosis, measures that show deviations from normality. A skewness value of 0 indicates a symmetric distribution about the mean; positive skewness values indicate a right-skewed distribution, and negative values indicate a left-skewed distribution. Left and right refer to the direction in which the elongated tail points. The value -.145 in this listing is very close to 0 and shows that there are no pronounced tails in the distribution of SBP. Kurtosis values indicate whether the distribution is more peaked than or flatter than a normal distribution. The value that SAS computes for kurtosis is scaled so that you get the value 0 for a normal distribution (also known as *relative kurtosis*). Positive values for kurtosis indicate both that the distribution is too peaked (leptokurtic) and that the tails are too heavy. Negative values for kurtosis indicate that the distribution is too flat (platykurtic) and that the tails are too light. The kurtosis value for SBP (-.535) indicates that the distribution of SBP is reasonably consistent with a normal distribution.

The coefficient of variation (often abbreviated CV) expresses the standard deviation as a percent of the mean. This output shows that the standard deviation is about 8.38% of the mean. Finally, the value at the bottom right of this section is the standard error of the mean (1.46), which gives you an estimate of how accurately this sample has estimated the population mean.

The remaining values in the section are less useful. This author believes that they were originally included so that you could use them in hand calculations of other statistics that were not computed by SAS. The sum of weights is useful only if you use a WEIGHT statement with PROC UNIVARIATE; with a WEIGHT statement you select a variable that weights the SBP values. In this example, because you did not specify any weights, the sum of weights is equal to the number of observations (all the weights are equal to 1). The uncorrected SS is the sum of squares of all the data values. To compute the corrected SS, you subtract the mean from each value before you square them, and then add them up. This value is the same as the numerator of the sample variance.

❷ The values listed in this section are somewhat redundant. They are grouped here for convenience as measures of location (mean, median, and mode) and measures of variability (standard deviation, variance, range, and interquartile range).

❸ This section displays a number of statistical tests that determine whether various measures of central location are significantly different from a theoretical value (mu). The default value for mu is mu=0. You can change the default value to another value by using the procedure option MU=n, where n is the nonzero value of your choice.

The tests listed in this section are a one-sample Student's *t*-test, a sign test, and a signed-rank test (also known as the Wilcoxon signed-rank test). These statistics are discussed in Chapter 5 (one-sample *t*-test) and Chapter 12 (the sign and Wilcoxon tests).

Quantiles (Definition 5) ❹	
Quantile	Estimate
100% Max	156
99%	156
95%	148
90%	144
75% Q3	138
50% Median	132
25% Q1	121
10%	114
5%	112
1%	108
0% Min	108

❹ Continuing the examination of the PROC UNIVARIATE output, you see a list of commonly used quantiles. The most useful values are the lowest value (0% Min), first quartile (25% Q1), median (50% Median), third quartile (75% Q3), and the maximum value (100% Max). If you supply PROC UNIVARIATE with some options, it can compute quantiles for any values you want, and write these values to a SAS data set.

| Extreme Observations ❺ | | | | | |
| Lowest | | | Highest | | |
Value	Subj	Obs	Value	Subj	Obs
108	56	56	144	54	54
110	60	60	146	8	8
112	48	48	148	44	44
112	47	47	150	3	3
114	51	51	156	18	18

| Missing Values ❻ | | | |
| Missing Value | Count | Percent Of | |
		All Obs	Missing Obs
.	4	6.67	100.00

❺ This section displays the five lowest and five highest values in your data set. You can quickly check the listed values to ensure that no values are dramatically different from what you expected (perhaps a data entry error occurred).

Because you used an ID statement, this portion of the output includes the Subj variable. The column labeled Obs is the observation number (which is not very useful because adding observations or sorting the data set will change the observation number). If you want to see more than the five lowest and five highest values, you can supply a procedure option NEXTROBS=n (number of extreme observations) to ask PROC UNIVARIATE to list any number of extreme observations.

❻ This section tells you how many observations had a missing value for the variable of interest. It also expresses this number as the percent of all your observations.

The HISTOGRAM and PROBPLOT statement both produce high quality SAS/GRAPH output. Depending on your system, these plots are either displayed immediately in your output window, or you need to click on the task bar at the bottom of your screen to see them. The following graph is the result of the HISTOGRAM statement:

Demonstrating PROC UNIVARIATE

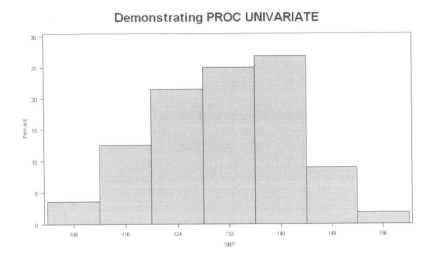

The x-axis shows ranges of SBP. The numbers that are displayed are the midpoints of the SBP ranges. The y-axis displays the percentage of values that fall within these ranges. In the next section, you will learn how to change these data ranges, but the values that SAS chooses for you are usually fine for a quick idea of what your distribution looks like. In this example, the SBP values look similar to those from a normal distribution.

The PROBPLOT statement produced the next graph:

Demonstrating PROC UNIVARIATE

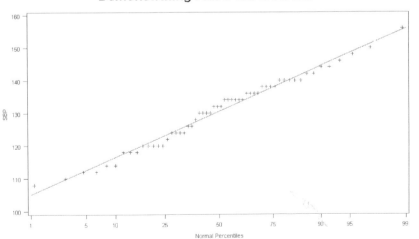

If your values came from a normal distribution, they would fall close to the diagonal line on the plot. In this example, the actual data points do not deviate much from this theoretical line, showing that the values of SBP come from a distribution that is close to normal. This outcome is also consistent with the values for skewness and kurtosis that you saw earlier.

Changing the Midpoint Values on the Histogram

If you want to change the midpoint values displayed on the histogram, you can supply a MIDPOINTS option on the HISTOGRAM statement. For example, if you want midpoints to go from 100 to 170 with each bin representing 5 points, you would write:

```
histogram / midpoints=100 to 170 by 5;
```

The following histogram used the MIDPOINTS option set to 100 to 170 by 5:

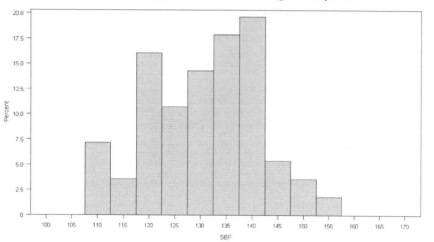

Finally, you could also see a theoretical normal curve superimposed on your histogram by including the NORMAL option on the HISTOGRAM statement like this:

```
histogram / midpoints=100 to 170 by 5 normal;
```

The output now shows a normal curve superimposed on your histogram:

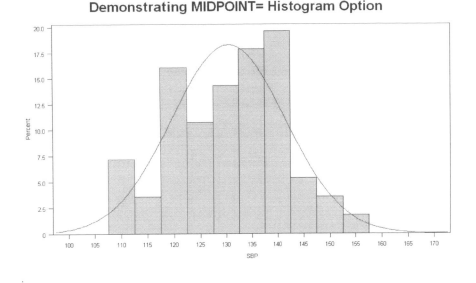

Demonstrating MIDPOINT= Histogram Option

Generating a Variety of Graphical Displays of Your Data

SAS 9.2 introduced several important and useful statistical graphics procedures. Among the more useful of these are SGPLOT and SGSCATTER. You can use SGPLOT to produce histograms, box plots, scatter plots, and much more. SGSCATTER displays several plots on a single page (including a scatter plot matrix that is particularly useful). The SG procedures come with a number of built-in styles. You can select different styles for your output without having to do any programming.

Let's see how to produce a histogram and a box plot using SGPLOT.

Program 2.6: Using PROC SGPLOT to Produce a Histogram

```
title "Using SGPLOT to Produce a Histogram";
proc sgplot data=example.Blood_Pressure;
   histogram SBP;
run;
```

This HISTOGRAM statement produces a histogram, similar in appearance to the histogram you obtained with the HISTOGRAM statement on PROC UNIVARIATE. As you will learn later, you can change the appearance of the output when you select alternate output destinations such as HTML, PDF, and RTF (rich text format), and one of the built-in styles.

First, let's see how to display the plot. Then you will learn a few of the more popular options that control the appearance of the output.

Output from the SG procedures does not usually open automatically after you run the procedure. One way to examine the output is to go to the Results window in SAS Display Manager:

You see the output from SGPLOT with a plus sign (+) to the left of it. Click the plus sign to expand the list:

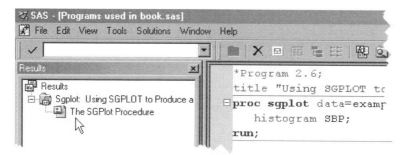

Now double click on the **SGPlot Procedure** icon to display the histogram. You can use this sequence of steps to display any of the graphs produced by the SG procedures or to display the plots produced by ODS Statistical Graphics that you will see later in this book.

Finally, after all this clicking, you will see your histogram:

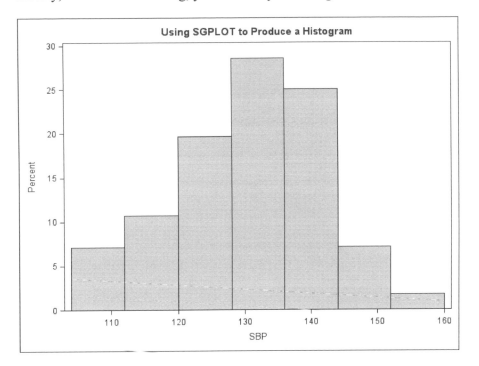

To produce a box-plot of the same data, use the HBOX statement (horizontal box plot) instead of the request for a histogram:

Program 2.7: Using SGPLOT to Produce a Horizontal Box Plot

```
title "Using SGPLOT to Produce a Box Plot";
proc sgplot data=example.Blood_Pressure;
   hbox SBP;
run;
```

Click your way through the Results window to see the following display:

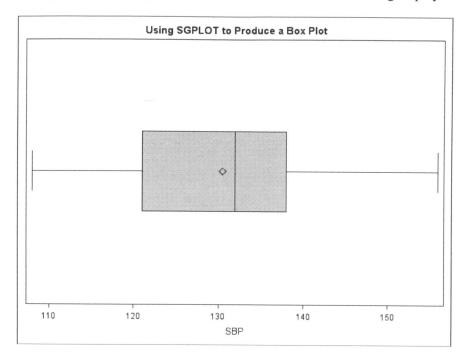

The left and right sides of the box represent the 1st and 3rd quartiles (sometimes abbreviated Q1 and Q3). The vertical bar inside the box is the median, and the diamond represents the mean. The lines extending from the left and right side of the box (called whiskers) represent data values that are less than 1.5 times the interquartile range from Q1 and Q3. If you prefer to see a vertical box plot, use the keyword VBOX instead of HBOX.

To see the effect of outliers on a box plot, let's modify two SBP values for subjects 5 and 55 to be 200 and 180, respectively. This modified data set is called `Blood_Pressure_Out` and is stored in the Work library (making it a temporary SAS data set). You can see the program to create this data set, as well as the request for the box plot, in Program 2.8:

Program 2.8: Displaying Outliers in a Box Plot

```
*Program to make a temporary SAS data set Blood_Pressure_Out that
contains two outliers, one for Subj 5, one for Subj 55;
data Blood_Pressure_Out;
   set example.Blood_Pressure(keep=Subj SBP);
   if Subj = 5 then SBP = 200;
   else if Subj = 55 then SBP = 180;
run;

title "Demonstrating How Outliers are Displayed with a Box
Plot";
proc sgplot data=Blood_Pressure_Out;
   hbox SBP;
run;
```

The SET statement is an instruction to read each of the observations from data set
example.Blood_Pressure. In parentheses following the data set name is a KEEP=
data set option. This option tells the program that you want only two of the variables
(Subj and SBP) to be read from the input data set. Finally, the IF-THEN statement is true
when the value of Subj is equal to 5. The assignment statement following the keyword
THEN is executed and the SBP value is set to 180. In a similar manner, the ELSE-IF
statement sets the value of SBP to 180 for subject 55.

The box plot of the modified data set shows the two outliers as small circles:

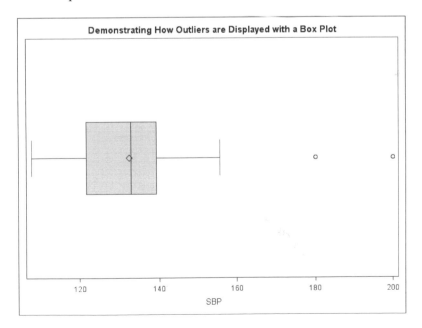

You can even get a bit fancier and let SAS label the outliers:

Program 2.9: Labeling Outliers on a Box Plot

```
title "Demonstrating How Outliers are Displayed with a Box Plot";
proc sgplot data=Blood_Pressure_Out;
   hbox SBP / datalabel=Subj;
run;
```

The option DATALABEL= lets you select a variable to identify specific outliers. If you use the DATALABEL option without naming a label variable, SGPLOT uses the numerical value of the response variable (SBP in this example) to label the outliers. Here is the output:

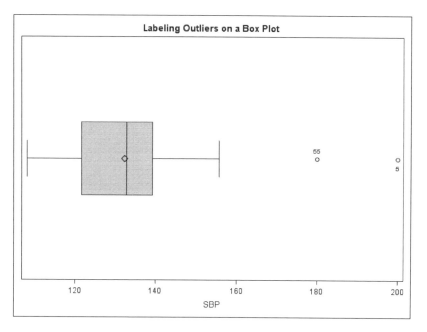

Notice that the outliers for subjects 5 and 55 are labeled.

Displaying Multiple Box Plots for Each Value of a Categorical Variable

If you want to see a box plot for each value of a categorical variable, you can include the option CATEGORY= on the HBOX or VBOX statement. The example that follows uses the original `Blood_Pressure` data set (without the outliers) and displays a box plot for each value of Drug.

Program 2.10: Displaying Multiple Box Plots for Each Value of a Categorical Variable

```
title "Box Plots of SBP for Each Value of Drug";
proc sgplot data=example.Blood_Pressure;
      hbox SBP / category=Drug;
run;
```

The HBOX option CATEGORY= generates a separate box plot for each of the three Drug values:

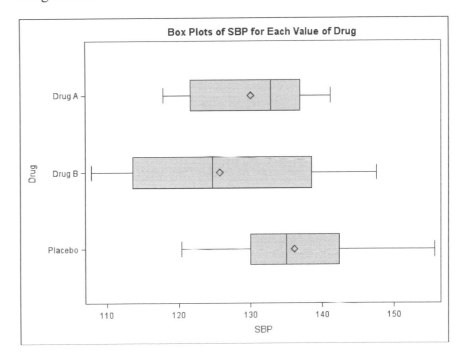

Conclusions

Descriptive statistics should be your first step in data analysis so that you can see a summary of the data and better understand their distribution. This chapter showed you how to produce both numerical and graphical output for continuous variables, using a number of SAS procedures.

The next two chapters will show you how to display descriptive statistics for categorical variables and how to investigate bivariate relationships.

40

Descriptive Statistics – Categorical Variables

Introduction

This chapter continues with methods of examining categorical variables. You will learn how to produce frequencies for single variables and then extend the process to create cross-tabulation tables. You will also learn several graphical approaches that are used with categorical variables. Finally, you will learn how to use SAS to group continuous variables into categories using a variety of techniques. Let's get started.

Computing Frequency Counts and Percentages

You can use PROC FREQ to count frequencies and calculate percentages for categorical variables. This procedure can count unique values for either character or numeric variables. Let's start by computing frequencies for Gender and Drug in the Blood_Pressure data set used in the previous chapter.

Program 3.1: Computing Frequencies and Percentages Using PROC FREQ

```
title "Computing Frequencies and Percentages Using PROC FREQ";
proc freq data=example.Blood_Pressure;
    tables Gender Drug;
run;
```

PROC FREQ uses a TABLES statement to identify which variables you want to process. This program selects Gender and Drug. Here is the output:

Computing Frequencies and Percentages Using PROC FREQ

The FREQ Procedure

Gender	Frequency	Percent	Cumulative Frequency	Cumulative Percent
F	28	48.28	28	48.28
M	30	51.72	58	100.00

Frequency Missing = 2

Drug	Frequency	Percent	Cumulative Frequency	Cumulative Percent
Drug A	20	33.33	20	33.33
Drug B	20	33.33	40	66.67
Placebo	20	33.33	60	100.00

By default, PROC FREQ computes frequencies, percentages, cumulative frequencies, and cumulative percentages. In addition, it reports the frequency of missing values. If you do not want all of these values, you can add options to the TABLES statement and specify what statistics you want or do not want. For example, if you want only frequencies and percentages, you can use the TABLES option NOCUM (no cumulative statistics) to remove them from the output, like this:

Program 3.2: Demonstrating the NOCUM Tables Option

```
title "Demonstrating the NOCUM Tables Option";
proc freq data=example.Blood_Pressure;
   tables Gender Drug / nocum;
run;
```

Because NOCUM is a statement option, it follows the usual SAS rule: it follows a slash. The following output shows the effect of the NOCUM option:

Demonstrating the NOCUM Tables Option

The FREQ Procedure

Gender	Frequency	Percent
F	28	48.28
M	30	51.72

Frequency Missing = 2

Drug	Frequency	Percent
Drug A	20	33.33
Drug B	20	33.33
Placebo	20	33.33

As you can see, the output now contains only frequencies and percents.

One TABLES option, MISSING, deserves special attention. This option tells PROC FREQ to treat missing values as a valid category and to include them in the body of the table. Program 3.3 shows the effect of including the MISSING option:

Program 3.3: Demonstrating the Effect of the MISSING Option with PROC FREQ

```
title "Demonstrating the effect of the MISSING Option";
proc freq data=example.Blood_Pressure;
   tables Gender Drug / nocum missing;
run;
```

Here is the output:

Demonstrating the effect of the MISSING Option

The FREQ Procedure

Gender	Frequency	Percent
	2	3.33
F	28	46.67
M	30	50.00

Drug	Frequency	Percent
Drug A	20	33.33
Drug B	20	33.33
Placebo	20	33.33

Notice that the two subjects with missing values for Gender are now included in the body of the table. Even more important, the percentages for females and males have changed. When you use the MISSING option, SAS treats missing values as a valid category and includes the missing values when it computes percentages. To summarize, without the MISSING option, percentages are computed as the percent of all nonmissing values; with the MISSING option, percentages are computed as the percent of all observations, missing and nonmissing.

Computing Frequencies on a Continuous Variable

What happens if you compute frequencies on a continuous numeric variable such as SBP (systolic blood pressure)? Program 3.4 shows what happens when you try to compute frequencies on a continuous numeric variable:

Program 3.4: Computing Frequencies on a Continuous Variable

```
title "Computing Frequencies on a Continuous Variable";
proc freq data=example.Blood_Pressure;
   tables SBP / nocum;
run;
```

This is the output:

Computing Frequencies on a Continuous Variable

The FREQ Procedure

SBP	Frequency	Percent
108	1	1.79
110	1	1.79
112	2	3.57
114	2	3.57
118	3	5.36
120	5	8.93
122	1	1.79
124	4	7.14
126	2	3.57
128	1	1.79
130	4	7.14
134	6	10.71
136	4	7.14
138	4	7.14
140	5	8.93
142	2	3.57
144	2	3.57
146	1	1.79
148	1	1.79
150	1	1.79
156	1	1.79

Frequency Missing = 4

Each unique value of SBP is considered a category. Now let's see how to group continuous values into categories.

Using Formats to Group Observations

SAS can apply formats to character or numeric variables. What is a format? Suppose you have been using M for males and F for females but you want to see the labels Male and Female in your output. You can create a format that associates any text (Male, for example) to one or more values. To demonstrate, let's start by making a format for Gender, SBP, and DBP, and using these formats with PROC FREQ.

Program 3.5: Writing a Format for Gender, SBP, and DBP

```
proc format;
   value $gender 'M' = 'Male'
                 'F' = 'Female';
   value sbpgroup low-140 = 'Normal'
         141-high        = 'High';
   value dbpgroup low-80 = 'Normal'
         81-high         = 'High';
run;

proc freq data=example.Blood_Pressure;
   tables Gender SBP DBP / nocum;
   format Gender $gender.
          SBP sbpgroup.
          DBP dbpgroup.;
run;
```

You use PROC FORMAT to create formats—labels associated with values. If you are planning to create formats for character variables, the format names must start with a dollar sign. Formats to be used with numeric variables cannot start with a dollar sign. In addition, format names cannot end with a number. All format names are limited to a maximum of 32 characters, including the initial dollar sign for character format names. Finally, format names can contain letters, digits, and the underscore character. You name each format on a VALUE statement. This statement lets you specify unique values, groups of values, or ranges of values on the left side of the equal sign, and labels that you want to associate with these values on the right side of the equal sign.

The first format in Program 3.5 is $gender. This name is a good choice because this format will be used later with the variable Gender (a character variable). All the format names are, however, completely arbitrary: you could have called this format $xyz if you wanted to. The $gender format associates the text "Male" with M and "Female" with F. You can use either single or double quotation marks when you create formats—just be sure to use double quotation marks if the format that you are creating contains an apostrophe (which is rendered as a single quotation mark).

The next two formats are to be used with the two variables SBP and DBP. For the SBPGROUP format, the range of values associated with the text "Normal" is from the lowest nonmissing value to 190. You can use the keywords LOW and HIGH when you are defining format ranges.

PROC FORMAT creates formats, but it does not associate any of these formats with SAS variables (even if you are clever and name them so that it is clear which format will go with which variable). To associate a format with one or more SAS variables, you use a FORMAT statement. You can place this statement in either a DATA step or a PROC step. If you place a FORMAT statement in a PROC step (as in Program 3.5), the format will be associated with the variables only for the duration of that procedure. If you place a FORMAT statement in a DATA step, the formats will be permanently assigned to the variables.

In a FORMAT statement, you start with the keyword FORMAT, followed by one or more variables names, followed by the format you want to associate with the variables you listed. On a FORMAT statement, you *must* follow each format name with a period. If you omit the period, SAS will think that you are writing a variable name and not a format. It is slightly confusing—when you create the format with a VALUE statement, you do not end the name with a period (SAS knows this is a format name). When you write a FORMAT statement, you must end the format name with a period.

Let's see what happens when you run Program 3.5—here is the output:

Computing Frequencies on a Continuous Variable

The FREQ Procedure

Gender	Frequency	Percent
Female	28	48.28
Male	30	51.72

Frequency Missing = 2

SBP	Frequency	Percent
Normal	48	85.71
High	8	14.29

Frequency Missing = 4

DBP	Frequency	Percent
Normal	24	42.86
High	32	57.14

Frequency Missing = 4

Instead of F's and M's you now see Female and Male. Instead of frequencies for individual values of SBP and DBP, you see only two categories, Normal and High.

Histograms and Bar Charts

Sometimes it is useful to show frequencies in a graphical display. With SAS, you have several options: First, there is an older SAS procedure called GCHART, which is part of the SAS/GRAPH collection of procedures. A newer procedure, PROC SGPLOT, can produce a wide variety of plots and charts.

The first example of a bar chart uses PROC GCHART to display the frequencies of a variable called Region (region of the country) from a data set called store. You can skip this section and go right to the next section, which shows you how to create a bar chart using PROC SGPLOT. However, at some point you might need to run or modify an older SAS program that uses PROC GCHART. Here is the code:

Program 3.6: Generating a Bar Chart Using PROC GCHART

```
goptions reset=all;
pattern value = solid color = blue;
title "Generating a Bar Chart - Using PROC GCHART";
proc gchart data=store;
   vbar Region;
run;
quit;
```

The first statement (GOPTIONS, which stands for graphic options), is not mandatory, but if you have been using any SAS/GRAPH procedures during your SAS session, it is a good idea to reset all the options to their default values. Why? Because when you set any graphic option such as color or plotting symbol, these options remain in effect until you change them. This behavior is similar to TITLE statements, which persist unless you change them or omit the titles completely.

The PATTERN statement enables you to select the type of bar (SOLID in this case) and the color of the bars. A useful hint is to set VALUE=EMPTY if you are sending the output to a dot matrix printer. The EMPTY option displays only the outline of the box and keeps you from rushing out to the office supply store to buy more ink cartridges.

The VBAR (vertical bar) statement lets you list the variables for which you want to generate bar charts. If you prefer a horizontal bar chart, use the HBAR statement instead.

Notice the QUIT statement in this program. Certain procedures in SAS such as PROC GCHART have something called RUN-group processing. This kind of processing keeps the procedure in memory, even after it encounters a RUN statement. Because the procedure is still in memory, you can request additional charts or, in the case of other procedures, new models, etc. The QUIT statement ends the procedure. If you omit a QUIT statement, the procedure ends when the next DATA or PROC step executes.

Here is the output from Program 3.6:

Generating a Bar Chart - Using PROC GCHART

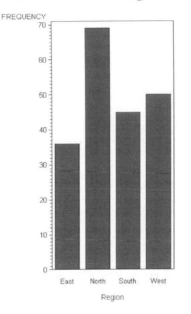

Creating a Bar Chart Using PROC SGPLOT

You can create a similar bar chart using PROC SGPLOT. A number of built-in styles make it very easy to customize your output. For example, a style called JOURNAL produces black and white output, suitable for publication in a journal. A style called STATISTICAL gives you output that is designed for statistical purposes.

Program 3.7 shows how to produce a chart similar to the one produced in Program 3.6:

Program 3.7: Generating a Bar Chart Using PROC SGPLOT

```
title "Generating a Bar Chart - Using PROC SGPLOT";
proc sgplot data=store;
   vbar Region;
run;
```

The syntax is almost identical to PROC GCHART. You enter the keyword VBAR, followed by one or more variables for which you want to create a bar chart. Here is the output:

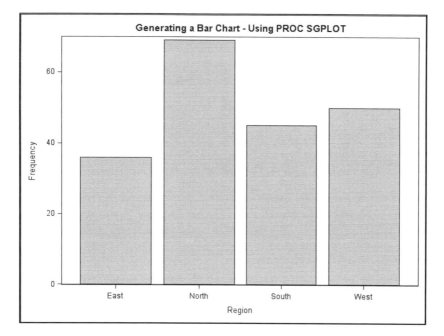

Using ODS to Send Output to Alternate Destinations

To demonstrate the flexibility of the SGPLOT procedure, the next example shows you how to use a built-in style to send the same chart to a PDF file.

Program 3.8: Using ODS to Create PDF Output

```
ods listing close;
ods pdf file='c:\books\statistics by example\bar.pdf'
       style=journal;
title "Generating a Bar Chart - Using PROC SGPLOT";
proc sgplot data=store;
   vbar Region;
run;
quit;
ods pdf close;
ods listing;
```

This program is identical to the previous one, except you place an ODS statement before the procedure that tells SAS two things: 1) you want to produce a PDF file and 2) you want to use the built-in style called JOURNAL. Following the procedure, you close the destination using another ODS statement.

You should close all your ODS destinations before you exit your SAS session. It is also a good idea to include the ODS LISTING CLOSE statement before the procedure so that you don't get two outputs—one sent to the PDF file and the other sent to the normal SAS output location. Remember that you need to reopen the listing file using the ODS LISTING statement following the procedure.

The PDF file that was created by Program 3.8 looks like this:

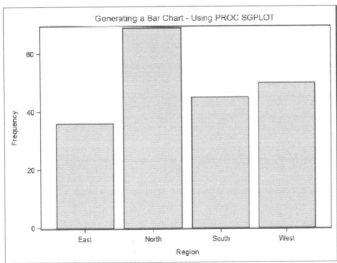
Generating a Bar Chart - Using PROC SGPLOT

This PDF file can be read by Adobe and used in any application that can work with PDF files.

Creating a Cross-Tabulation Table

You can use PROC FREQ to create a cross-tabulation table. You start out with the keyword TABLES. Following this, you specify the two variables of interest, separated by an asterisk. For example, the `store` data set contains the variables Region and Gender. If you want to see the distribution of Gender across all values of Region, you proceed with Program 3.9:

Program 3.9: Creating a Cross-Tabulation Table Using PROC FREQ

```
title "Demonstrating a Cross-Tabulation Table using PROC FREQ";
proc freq data=store;
   tables Gender * Region;
run;
```

This program requests a table of Gender by Region. In this example, Gender will form the rows of the table, and Region will form the columns.

The general form of a cross-tabulation request is:

```
tables  row-variable * column-variable;
```

Here is the output from Program 3.9:

Demonstrating a Cross-Tabulation Table using PROC FREQ

The FREQ Procedure

Frequency Percent Row Pct Col Pct	Table of Gender by Region				
		Region			
Gender	East	North	South	West	Total
Female	22	39	23	26	110
	11.00	19.50	11.50	13.00	55.00
	20.00	35.45	20.91	23.64	
	61.11	56.52	51.11	52.00	
Male	14	30	22	24	90
	7.00	15.00	11.00	12.00	45.00
	15.56	33.33	24.44	26.67	
	38.89	43.48	48.89	48.00	
Total	36	69	45	50	200
	18.00	34.50	22.50	25.00	100.00

Each box in the table contains four values; the meaning of these values is found in the key in the upper-left corner of the table. As you can see, the top number in each box is the number of observations. For example, there are 22 females in the Eastern region. The next number is a percentage. In this example, 11% of all observations are females in the Eastern region. The third number in each box is a row percentage—20% of the females were in the Eastern region. Finally, the fourth number in each box is a column percentage; 61.11% of the observations from the Eastern region are female.

Notice the order of the rows and columns in the output. By default, SAS orders the rows and columns in a table (or for a single variable) by the internal value of the variable—alphabetically for character variables and numerically for numeric variables. This is why the rows in the previous table were ordered Female→Male and the order of the columns was East→North→South→West.

Changing the Order of Values in a Frequency Table

Whether you have a one-way or a two-way table, you might want to control the order that SAS uses for the rows, the columns, or both. In the previous example, maybe you want the regions to be ordered North→East→South→West. Or you might be computing an odds ratio in a 2x2 table and want the first column to be labeled Yes and the second column to be labeled No.

You can accomplish these goals in several ways. One is to create a new variable from the existing variable, where the internal values are in the desired order. Another, easier, method is to associate formats that are in the target order and associate that format with your variable. You can then use a PROC FREQ option called ORDER=FORMATTED to tell SAS to order the rows, columns, or both by their formatted values, rather than by their internal values.

The example that follows uses this method to force the order of the regions to be North, East, South, and West. First the program, then the explanation.

Program 3.10: **Changing the Order of Values in a PROC FREQ Table By Using Formats**

```
proc format;
   value $region 'North' = '1 North'
                 'East'  = '2 East'
                 'South' = '3 South'
                 'West'  = '4 West';
run;

title "Change the Order in a PROC FREQ Output";
proc freq data=store order=formatted;
   tables Gender * Region;
   format Region region.;
run;
```

The four formatted values created by the $region format are in the desired order alphabetically. (Note that the digits 1, 2, 3, and 4 are part of the format labels, and 1 comes before 2 alphabetically, etc.) Including a FORMAT statement in PROC FREQ associates the $region format with the variable called Region. (Remember that the association is made by the FORMAT statement, not because the name of the format is similar to the name of the variable.) Finally, to tell SAS to order the table by the formatted values rather than by the internal values, you must include the PROC FREQ option ORDER=FORMATTED.

Here is the output from Program 3.10:

Change the Order in a PROC FREQ Output

The FREQ Procedure

Frequency Percent Row Pct Col Pct	Table of Gender by Region				
		Region			
Gender	1 North	2 East	3 South	4 West	Total
Female	39	22	23	26	110
	19.50	11.00	11.50	13.00	55.00
	35.45	20.00	20.91	23.64	
	56.52	61.11	51.11	52.00	
Male	30	14	22	24	90
	15.00	7.00	11.00	12.00	45.00
	33.33	15.56	24.44	26.67	
	43.48	38.89	48.89	48.00	
Total	69	36	45	50	200
	34.50	18.00	22.50	25.00	100.00

The regions are now ordered 1 North, 2 East, 3 South, and 4 West. Because female comes before male alphabetically, the order is Female, then Male.

Conclusions

In this chapter, you learned how to display values of categorical variables, both in tabular and graphical form. Although you can use several methods to change the order of rows and columns in a table, using formats might be the simplest.

You also learned how to use the built-in styles to create attractive output with a minimum of effort. And you saw how to use ODS to send this output to a variety of destinations, such as HTML, PDF, and RTF.

The next chapter finishes up our discussion of descriptive statistics by showing you how to produce numerical and graphical displays for bivariate relationships.

56

Descriptive Statistics – Bivariate Associations

Introduction

This chapter introduces you to some graphical methods for displaying relationships between two continuous variables. First are simple scatter plots that were produced with several different procedures. Next, you will learn how to create multiple plots on a single page using PROC SGSCATTER.

All of the examples in this chapter use data from the `store` data set. This data set contains the following variables:

Variable Name	Type	Description
Region	Character	Region of the country (North, East, South, West)
Advertising	Character	Advertising (Yes or No)
Gender	Character	Gender of shopper (M or F)
Book_Sales	Numeric	Amount spent on books
Music_Sales	Numeric	Amount spent on music
Electronics_Sales	Numeric	Amount spent on electronics
Total_Sales	Numeric	Total sales

Producing a Simple Scatter Plot Using PROG GPLOT

You can produce a scatter plot using either the GPLOT or SGPLOT procedure. Both are part of the SAS/GRAPH package. The next section in this chapter shows you how to produce scatter plots using the newer SGPLOT procedure, which is the recommended method for making scatter plots. This section is included mainly so that you will understand programs that were written before PROC SGPLOT was available.

By supplying a few graphics options, you can control the appearance of the plot. The first program uses PROC GPLOT to plot Book_Sales by Music_Sales.

Program 4.1: Creating a Scatter Plot Using PROC GPLOT

```
title "Creating a Scatter Plot Using PROC GPLOT";
symbol value=dot;
proc gplot data=store;
   plot Book_Sales * Music_Sales;
run;
quit;
```

The SYMBOL statement before the PROC GPLOT statement is a global graphics instruction that tells the procedure to use dots as the plotting symbol. Without this statement, the procedure uses the default plotting symbol, a plus sign. You specify the variables to be plotted, using a PLOT statement. This statement takes the following form:

```
plot y-variable * x-variable;
```

You can include spaces before and after the asterisk if you want or you can leave them out—your choice.

Here is the plot:

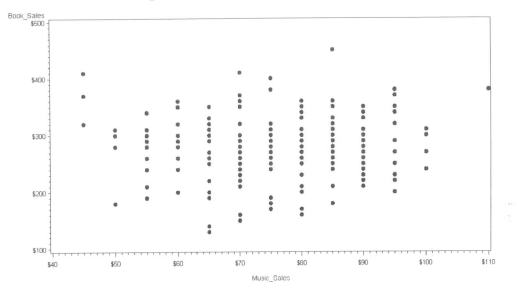

Suppose you want to see this same plot, but with Gender identified. You can modify your plot to include Gender information like this:

Program 4.2: Adding Gender Information to the Plot

```
goptions reset=all;
title "Creating a Scatter Plot Using PROC GPLOT";
title2 "Adding Gender Information to the Plot";
symbol1 color=black value=dot;
symbol2 color=black value=square;
proc gplot data=store;
   plot Book_Sales * Music_Sales = Gender;
run;
quit;
```

A few new statements have been added to this program. First, notice the GOPTIONS (pronounced by most folks as gee-options). Because graphics options stay in effect until you change them, it is a good idea to reset all the graphics options back to their default values before producing a new graph. GOPTIONS does this for you.

This program also has two TITLE statements. The second TITLE statement is written as TITLE2. As you can probably guess, TITLE2 causes a second title line to be printed. You can write up to ten TITLE statements. (TITLE and TITLE1 are equivalent.) All titles stay in effect until you change or cancel them. If you write a new TITLE*n* statement, all TITLE statements below that are removed. For example, if you were to write a new program following Program 4.2 and included a new TITLE statement, the old TITLE2 line definition would be removed.

This program also defines two SYMBOL statements (SYMBOL1 and SYMBOL2), with plotting symbols of dots and squares, respectively. Finally, the PLOT statement is in the following form:

```
plot Book_Sales * Music_Sales = Gender;
```

You follow the y by x plot request with an equal sign and your grouping variable—in this case, Gender. Each unique value of Gender will be displayed with a different plotting symbol. Looking at the output should make this clear. In particular, look at the legend below the scatter plot.

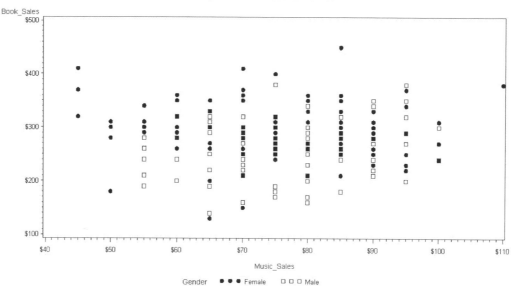

Producing a Scatter Plot Using PROC SGPLOT

You have already seen PROC SGPLOT used to produce histograms, box plots, and bar charts. You can use this same procedure to produce scatter plots by using the SCATTER statement like this:

Program 4.3: Using PROC SGPLOT to Produce a Scatter Plot

```
title "Using PROC SGPLOT to Produce a Scatter Plot";
proc sgplot data=store;
    scatter x=Book_Sales y=Music_Sales;
run;
quit;
```

Following the keyword SCATTER, you specify the variable you want on the x-axis and the variable you want on the y-axis. You can specify the x and y variables in any order. This program produces the following output:

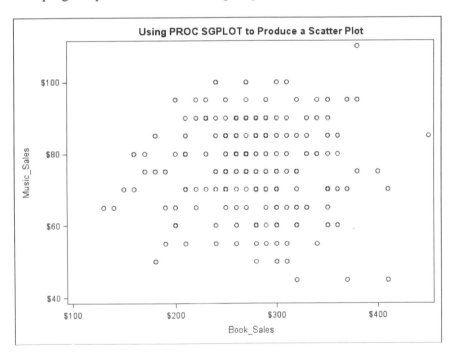

The plotting symbols on this plot are circles (the default symbol). The SG procedures do not use a global SYMBOL statement—you can specify symbols with options. For example, if you want filled-in triangles as plotting symbols, you could request them like this:

```
scatter x=Book_Sales y=Music_Sales /
   markerattrs=(symbol=trianglefilled);
```

You can find a list of plotting symbols in the help menu for each Statistical Graphics (SG) procedure.

You can produce a graph that includes gender information by adding a GROUP= option like this:

Program 4.4: Adding Gender to the Scatter Plot Using PROC SGPLOT

```
title "Using PROC SGPLOT to Produce a Scatter Plot";
title2 "Adding Gender Information to the Plot";
proc sgplot data=store;
   scatter x=Book_Sales y=Music_Sales / group=Gender;
run;
quit;
```

Including the option GROUP=Gender adds gender information to the plot, as shown in the following scatter plot. (Circles and plus signs as plotting symbols are the defaults for this procedure.)

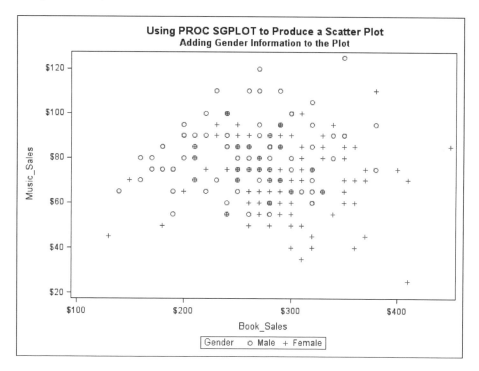

Creating Multiple Scatter Plots on a Single Page Using PROC SGSCATTER

You can use PROC SGSCATTER to display multiple plots on a single page. A PLOT statement lets you produce separate scatter plots on a single page. A COMPARE statement creates plots of one variable versus several variables on a single page. Finally, a MATRIX statement generates a scatter plot matrix. This section contains an example of each of these plots.

The PLOT Statement: Generating More than One Plot on a Page

The next program shows you how to use a PLOT statement to produce two scatter plots on a single page. One of the plots shows Book_Sales by Music_Sales; the other shows Total_Sales by Electronics_Sales. Here is the program:

Program 4.5: Demonstrating the PLOT Statement of PROC SGSCATTER

```
title "Demonstrating the PLOT Statement of PROC SGSCATTER";
proc sgscatter data=store;
    plot Book_Sales * Music_Sales  Total_Sales * Electronics_Sales;
run;
```

Following the PLOT keyword, you can specify multiple plots using this form

```
plot y-var1*x-var1  y-var2*x-var2 … y-varn*x-varn;
```

Each of these plots will be displayed on the same page, as shown in the following graph.

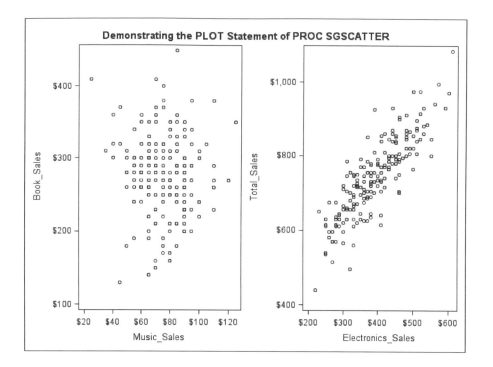

The COMPARE Statement: Plotting One Variable versus Several Variables on a Single Page

Suppose you want to see the variable Total_Sales (from the `store` data set) versus each of the variables Book_Sales, Music_Sales, and Electronics_Sales. You use PROC SGSCATTER with a COMPARE statement to do this, as shown in Program 4.6:

Program 4.6: Demonstrating the COMPARE Statement of PROC SGSCATTER

```
title "Comparing Total Sales to Book, Music, and Electronics Sales";
proc sgscatter data=store;
   compare y=Total_Sales x=(Book_Sales Music_Sales Electronics_Sales);
run;
```

In this example, Total_Sales is on the y-axis and each of the three other variables is on the x-axis. Notice that the three x-variables are placed in parentheses. The main difference between PLOT and COMPARE is that COMPARE uses a common axis (hence uniform data ranges) for one of the axes and PLOT does not. The following plot is the result:

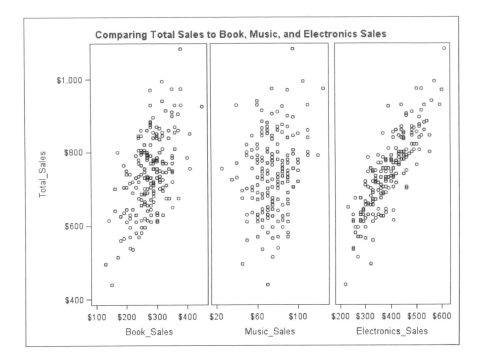

You can reverse the x- and y-axis requests if you prefer to see Total_Sales on the x-axis. You can also use the GROUP= option as you did earlier with PROC SGPLOT to identify which data points were from males and which were from females.

The next program demonstrates switching the axes and including the GROUP= option:

Program 4.7: Switching the x- and y-Axes and Adding a GROUP= Option

```
title "Switching Axes and Adding a GROUP= Option";
proc sgscatter data=store;
   compare x=Total_Sales
           y=(Book_Sales Music_Sales Electronics_Sales) /
              group=Gender;
run;
```

This program produces the following result:

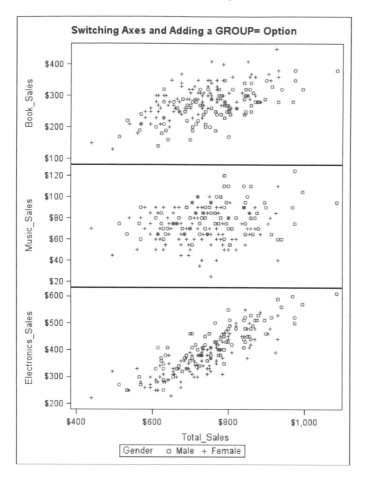

Because you specified only one x variable and three y variables, the plots are stacked vertically. The GROUP= option caused different plotting symbols to be used to identify males and females.

As a final note, you can list more than one variable on both the x- and y-axes. When you specify more than one variable on a given axis, remember to place the list of variables in parentheses.

If you prefer to see every variable compared to every other variable, you can use a MATRIX statement, as demonstrated in the next section.

The MATRIX Statement: Creating a Scatter Plot Matrix

If you want to see a matrix of scatter plots (every variable versus every other variable), you can use a MATRIX statement with PROC SGSCATTER. As a simple example, the next program produces a scatter matrix for the three `store` variables Book_Sales, Music_Sales, and Electronics_Sales.

Program 4.8: Producing a Scatter Plot Matrix

```
title "Producing a Scatter Plot Matrix";
proc sgscatter data=store;
   matrix Book_Sales Music_Sales Electronics_Sales /
      diagonal=(histogram);
run;
```

In this program, the variable list follows the keyword MATRIX. If you include too many variables in this list, the plots will be very small and not very useful. You might want to limit the number of variables to 5 or fewer.

By default, the plots on the diagonal show the variable names. Program 4.8 includes a DIAGONAL= option, as well as the HISTOGRAM option. The plots on the diagonal will contain a histogram of each of your variables. You can include other diagonal options in the parentheses, such as NORMAL (adds a normal curve to the histogram), or KERNEL (adds a kernel density line to the histogram).

Here is the output from Program 4.8:

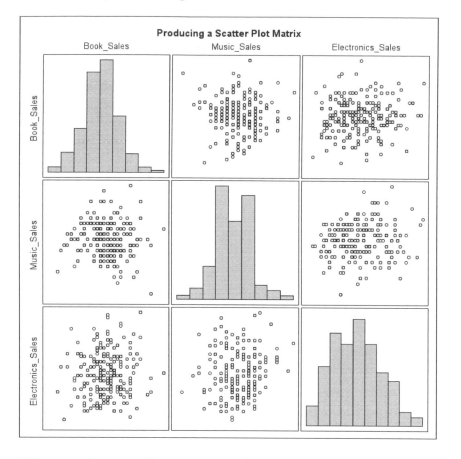

This output is an excellent way to see the relationships among several variables and the individual distributions in one display.

Conclusions

In this chapter, you learned how to create simple scatter plots using both the older PROC GPLOT and the newer PROC SGPLOT. In addition, you saw several ways to place multiple plots on one page, using PROC SGSCATTER and a PLOT, COMPARE, or MATRIX statement.

This chapter ends the descriptive statistics portion of this book. In the chapters that follow, you will learn how to produce most of the commonly used statistical methods for testing inferences.

Inferential Statistics –
One-Sample Tests

Introduction

This is the first chapter in the Inferential Statistics section of the book. This chapter shows you how to conduct a one-sample *t*-test using several methods. In addition, you will see how to test the assumption of normally distributed data.

This chapter also demonstrates how to specify plots using ODS Statistical Graphics (referred to as ODS Graphics) and how to use the built-in SAS documentation to learn how to customize the plots that SAS produces.

You will be using the `exercise` data set for the examples in this chapter. The following variables are in this data set:

Variable Name	Type	Description
Subj	Numeric	Subject number
Age	Numeric	Age in years
Pushups	Numeric	Number of pushups subject can do
Rest_Pulse	Numeric	Resting pulse rate
Max_Pulse	Numeric	Maximum pulse rate
Run_Pulse	Numeric	Pulse rate while running

PROC TTEST can perform one-sample *t*-tests, two-sample unpaired *t*-tests, and two-sample paired *t*-tests. This procedure automatically tests the assumption of homogeneity of variance for two sample designs and computes t- and p-values for the assumptions of equal or unequal variances. If you use ODS Graphics, you can produce different types of diagnostic and summary plots.

Because you might need to run or modify older SAS programs, you will see some of the older methods for performing a one-sample *t*-test later in this chapter.

Conducting a One-Sample *t*-test Using PROC TTEST

Suppose you want to test whether the age of your subjects in the `exercise` data set might reasonably be assumed to come from a population with a mean of 50. You could write the following program:

Program 5.1: Conducting a One-Sample *t*-test Using PROC TTEST

```
title "Conducting a One-Sample t-test Using PROC TTEST";
proc ttest data=exercise h0=50 sides=2 alpha=.05;
   var Age;
run;
```

In this program, you specify the null hypothesis with the H0= option on the procedure statement. In this example, you have specified that this is to be a two-sided test (also known as a two-tailed test) with ALPHA=.05. Conducting a two-sided test and setting alpha to .05 are the defaults for this procedure, so including these options is optional. If you want to conduct a one-sided test or change the value of ALPHA, you can use these two options to do that. For example, you can enter SIDES=U or SIDES=L if you want to conduct a one-sided test in the upper tail (U) or lower tail (L). You can also specify other values for ALPHA such as ALPHA=.10.

Here is the output:

Conducting a One-Sample *t*-test Using PROC TTEST

Variable: Age

N	Mean	Std Dev	Std Err	Minimum	Maximum
50	51.3600	16.1419	2.2828	19.0000	84.0000

Mean	95% CL Mean		Std Dev	95% CL Std Dev	
51.3600	46.7725	55.9475	16.1419	13.4839	20.1150

DF	t Value	Pr > |t|
49	0.60	0.5541

On the first line, you see the mean, standard deviation, standard error, minimum and maximum for Age. On the next line, you see the mean and its 95% confidence interval (also known as 95% confidence limits, hence the abbreviation CL) and the standard deviation and its 95% confidence interval. Finally, on the last line, you see the t-value (.60) along with the probability for a two-tailed test (p=.5541). If you set ALPHA equal to .05, you would declare this result as not significant.

Running PROC TTEST with ODS Graphics Turned On

If you want to see some automatic summary and diagnostic plots, you can rerun Program 5.1 with ODS Graphics turned on, like this:

Program 5.2: Demonstrating ODS Graphics with PROC TTEST

```
ods graphics on;
title "Demonstrating the Default ODS Graphics for PROC TTEST";
proc ttest data=exercise h0=50 sides=2 alpha=.05;
   var Age;
run;
ods graphics off;
```

You turn on ODS Graphics with the ODS GRAPHICS ON statement and you turn it off with the ODS GRAPHICS OFF statement. If you do not turn ODS Graphics off and you run more statistical procedures, those procedures also create ODS Graphics plots. In this example, the graphics turn off after the procedure runs.

The PRINTED output from this program is identical to that of Program 5.1. Two plots are created, by default when you request a one-sample *t*-test and turn on ODS Graphics. These plots do not appear automatically. The easiest way to see all of the plots produced by ODS Graphics is to do the following steps:

1. Right-click on the Ttest icon.

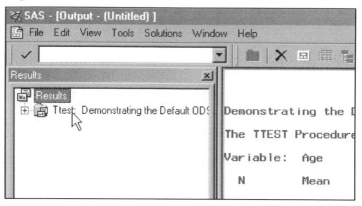

2. Select **Expand All** in the drop-down menu.

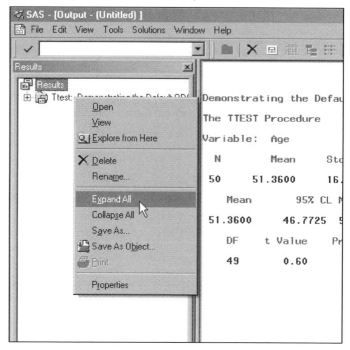

3. Select the plot you want to view.

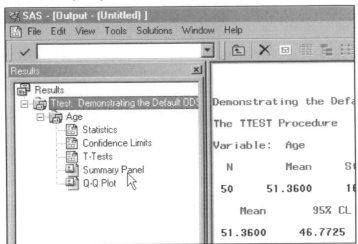

Here is the first plot that Program 5.2 produces:

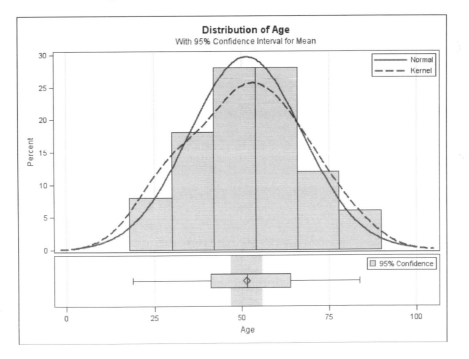

This first plot is called a Summary Panel. It shows a histogram for your dependent variable (Age) as well as a box plot for Age and its 95% confidence interval.

The next plot produced by ODS Graphics is a Q-Q (quantile-quantile) plot of the dependent variable, Age. This plot shows ordered values of your variable on the y-axis and quantiles from a normal distribution on the x-axis. If your data values are normally distributed, the points on the Q-Q plot should cluster around the diagonal line on the plot.

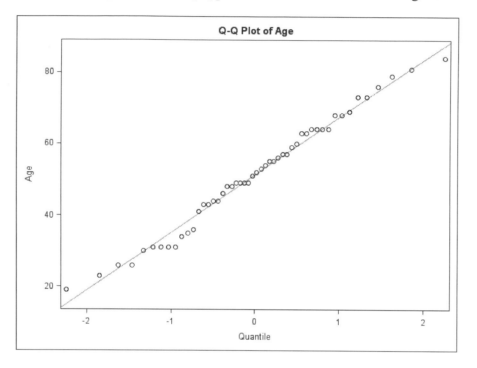

Because the data points closely follow the straight diagonal line, your Age values are consistent with a normal distribution.

Conducting a One-Sample *t*-test Using PROC UNIVARIATE

PROC UNIVARIATE is not the most up-to-date way to conduct a one-sample t-test. The decision to include this older method of conducting a one-sample *t*-test was two-fold: First, you might need to run or modify older programs that used this method to conduct one-sample *t*-tests. The other reason is that using PROC UNIVARIATE produces a data set of values that you can test for normality.

If you run PROC UNIVARIATE without any procedure options, part of your output contains several statistical tests that compare each variable in your VAR list against zero. The next program produces that kind of output.

Program 5.3: Conducting a One-Sample *t*-test

```
title "Conducting a One-Sample t-test";
proc univariate data=exercise;
   var Age;
   id Subj;
run;
```

The following section shows the output of interest:

Tests for Location: Mu0=0				
Test		Statistic	p Value	
Student's t	t	22.49856	Pr > |t|	<.0001
Sign	M	25	Pr >= |M|	<.0001
Signed Rank	S	637.5	Pr >= |S|	<.0001

By default, PROC UNIVARIATE tests the assumption that your sample came from a population with a mean of zero (labeled Mu0=0 in the output). The results of a one-sample *t*-test are displayed first. In this example, the t-value was about 22.5 and the p-value was listed as <.0001. The two other statistical tests shown on this output are a sign test and a Wilcoxon signed-rank test. You can read about these non-parametric tests in Chapter 12.

To test a null hypothesis that the sample came from a population with a given mean, you need to include the procedure option MU=*value*. For example, to test that the sample came from a population with a mean of 50, you would write:

Program 5.4: Conducting a One-Sample Test with a Nonzero Null Hypothesis

```
title "Conducting a One-Sample t-test with a Given Population
Mean";
proc univariate data=exercise mu0=50;
   var Age;
   id Subj;
run;
```

The only change in this program is the option MU0=50. Here is the portion of the output that shows the test for location:

Tests for Location: Mu0=50				
Test	Statistic		p Value	
Student's t	t	0.595756	Pr > |t|	0.5541
Sign	M	1	Pr >= |M|	0.8877
Signed Rank	S	52	Pr >= |S|	0.6204

In this example, you would fail to reject the null hypothesis that μ=50, using any one of the statistical tests. Notice that the t- and p-values are identical to the ones produced by PROC TTEST in Program 5.1.

Testing Whether a Distribution is Normally Distributed

You might need to test whether a sample comes from a population that is normally distributed. Another reason you might need to test normal assumptions is to inspect your residuals from an ANOVA or regression model.

You have already learned how to create a probability plot and a Q-Q plot using PROC UNIVARIATE. If you include the procedure option NORMAL, SAS includes several tests for normality.

Program 5.5 shows how to test whether age, from the `exercise` data set, is normally distributed.

Program 5.5: Testing Whether a Variable is Normally Distributed

```
title "Testing if a Variable is Normally Distributed";
proc univariate data=exercise normal;
   var Age;
   probplot / normal (mu=est sigma=est);
run;
```

Besides including the NORMAL option to conduct the various statistical tests, you can include a request for a probability plot as in this example. Here is the portion of the output that displays the tests for normality:

Tests for Normality				
Test	Statistic		p Value	
Shapiro-Wilk	W	0.981706	Pr < W	0.6258
Kolmogorov-Smirnov	D	0.076402	Pr > D	>0.1500
Cramer-von Mises	W-Sq	0.033844	Pr > W-Sq	>0.2500
Anderson-Darling	A-Sq	0.253843	Pr > A-Sq	>0.2500

All of the tests shown in this output result in a decision of fail to reject H_0. In practice, these tests for normality can produce dramatically different results.

The probability plot, which is shown next, also supports the idea that the sample came from a normal distribution.

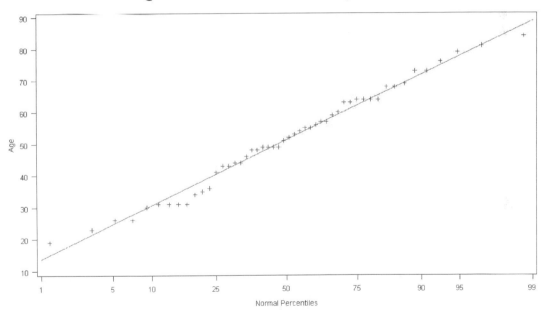

Testing if a Variable is Normally Distributed

A word of warning concerning these tests for normality: whether or not these tests are useful is not always clear. When you have a large number of observations, the tests for normality are usually significant, even if the deviations from normality are small; when you have a small number of observations, the tests for normality are usually non-significant, because of the low power. However, when you have a large sample size, the normality assumptions are usually not that important; when you have a small sample size, deviations from normality can be quite important.

Tests for Other Distributions

Whether you request probability plots or Q-Q plots (using a QQPLOT statement), you can specify several other distributions:

- normal (default)
- beta
- exponential
- gamma
- lognormal
- two-parameter Weibull
- three-parameter Weibull

For example, to test whether your distribution of ages comes from a three-parameter Weibull distribution, you would write your PROBPLOT (or QQPLOT) statement like this:

```
probplot Age / weibull (c=est);
```

Most of the distributions require you to specify values for the appropriate parameters. See the SAS OnlineDoc for details concerning these parameters.

Conclusions

In this first chapter on inferential statistics, you learned how to conduct a one-sample *t*-test using PROC TTEST and PROC UNIVARIATE. Invoking ODS Statistical Graphics prior to running PROC TTEST provides you with some useful plots that can help you decide whether normality assumptions required for a *t*-test have been met.

In the next chapter, you will see how to run two-sample *t*-tests, for both unpaired and paired data.

Inferential Statistics – Two-Sample Tests

Introduction

This chapter covers most of the popular two-sample tests, for paired and unpaired samples. If the assumptions for these tests are not met, SAS provides several non-parametric tests that are covered in Chapter 12.

Conducting a Two-Sample *t*-test

Let's start with a simple two-sample, unpaired *t*-test. For this example, you will compare the systolic blood pressure (SBP) and diastolic blood pressure (DBP) between the males and females (Gender) in the `blood_pressure` data set.

Here is the program:

Program 6.1: Conducting a Two-Sample *t*-test

```
title "Conducting a Two-Sample T-test";
proc ttest data=example.blood_pressure;
   class Gender;
   var SBP DBP;
run;
```

You name your independent variable on a CLASS statement. Only one CLASS variable is allowed and this variable must have exactly two nonmissing values. You name one or more dependent variables on a VAR statement. PROC TTEST conducts a separate *t*-test for each variable that you list on the VAR statement. The order of the CLASS and VAR statements does not matter.

Here is the output (for SBP only):

The TTEST Procedure

Variable: SBP ❶

Gender	N	Mean	Std Dev	Std Err	Minimum	Maximum
F	28	129.5	10.8951	2.0590	108.0	148.0
M	26	130.5	10.2654	2.0132	112.0	150.0
Diff (1-2) ❷		-0.9615	10.5970	2.8861		

Gender	Method	Mean	95% CL Mean ❸		Std Dev	95% CL Std Dev	
F		129.5	125.3	133.7	10.8951	8.6139	14.8298
M		130.5	126.3	134.6	10.2654	8.0507	14.1705
Diff (1-2)	Pooled ❹	-0.9615	-6.7530	4.8299	10.5970	8.8947	13.1114
Diff (1-2)	Satterthwaite	-0.9615	-6.7400	4.8170			

Method ❺	Variances	DF	t Value	Pr > |t|
Pooled	Equal	52	-0.33	0.7404
Satterthwaite	Unequal	51.987	-0.33	0.7398

Equality of Variances ❻				
Method	Num DF	Den DF	F Value	Pr > F
Folded F	27	25	1.13	0.7679

Let's examine the output. ❶ The first section gives you the mean, standard deviation, and several other statistics for the dependent variable, SBP. ❷ The mean difference in SBP between the males and females was -.9615 (females minus males). The standard error of the difference was 2.8861. ❸ The second section shows the 95% confidence interval for each mean, as well as the 95% confidence interval for the standard deviation. ❹ The 95% confidence interval for the mean difference is computed two ways: one under the assumption of equal variance (labeled Pooled) and the other under the assumption of unequal variance (labeled Satterthwaite). ❺ The third section displays the t-value and the associated probabilities. ❻ The last portion of the *t*-test output is a test for equality of variances. In this example, you fail to reject the null hypothesis that the samples came from populations with equal variances (p=.7679).

The decision to choose the pooled or Satterthwaite values is somewhat controversial. Some statisticians recommend that you look at the p-value from the test for equality of variances to decide which t- and p-value to use. Others think that this is somewhat circular reasoning and that you should decide ahead of time which assumption is most reasonable.

Testing the Assumptions for a *t*-test

The *t*-test procedure automatically conducts the homogeneity of variance assumption for you. If you want to determine whether the residuals are normally distributed, you have several choices. By far the easiest is to let SAS do it for you and request the ODS Statistical Graphics option. All you need to do is to insert the statement `ods graphics on;` before you run the procedure and `ods graphics off;` when you are done. If you do not turn it off, SAS will produce ODS Statistical Graphics for any subsequent procedures that support such graphics.

When you request ODS Graphics, PROC TTEST automatically produces some useful diagnostics. If you want or need more control of the output, you can add a PLOTS= option on the PROC TTEST statement to request specific plots. Let's start by seeing what you get when you turn on statistical graphics.

Program 6.2: Demonstrating ODS Graphics

```
ods graphics on;
title "Conducting a Two-Sample T-test";
proc ttest data=example.blood_pressure;
    class Gender;
    var SBP DBP;
run;
ods graphics off;
```

The listing output is the same as that produced by Program 6.1, so let's focus on the additional plots produced by ODS Graphics. Remember, the plots that are created are not displayed automatically. You need to right-click the **Ttest** icon in the Results window and select **Expand All**. (See the screen captures in Chapter 5 if you need to review this procedure.)

The first plot that is produced is labeled Summary Panel. This panel contains a histogram, with a superimposed normal curve for each of the genders. Below these histograms is a box plot of SBP for each value of Gender:

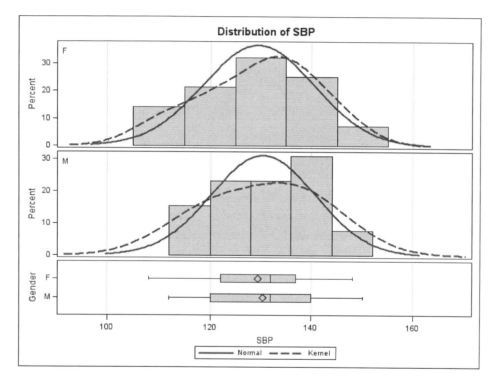

You can see from this plot that there is very little difference in SBP by gender.

To inspect the distribution of SBP for each value of Gender, ODS Graphics produces a Q-Q plot of SBP for each value of Gender:

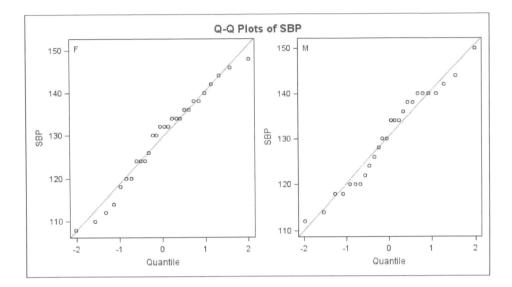

By looking at these plots, you would most likely conclude that the SBP does not deviate markedly from a normal distribution.

Customizing the Output from ODS Statistical Graphics

You can request specific plots from ODS Graphics. You do this by including a PLOTS= option when you run any procedure that produces statistical graphics.

The first step is to determine what plot options are available for the procedure that you are going to run. For example, to see what plot options are available with PROC TTEST, you can refer to the *SAS/STAT 9.2 User's Guide* (available from SAS Publishing) or use the online documentation that comes with SAS.

To use the online documentation to see the PLOT options for PROC TTEST:

1. On the command line, click the help icon ⬛. A menu of items appears.
2. Click on the small + sign to the left of **SAS Products** (at the bottom of the list) to expand the list of products.
3. Double-click **SAS PROCEDURES**.
4. In the main window to the right, click **T** in the alphabet list to navigate to the SAS procedures that start with the letter T.

5. Click **TTEST**.

6. Select **ODS Graphics** to see all of the plots available for the TTEST procedure.

You can now see what the default plots are for each type of *t*-test you perform (the plots differ depending on whether you are conducting a one-sample test, a paired test, etc.)

There are options for most of the plots, as well as global options that affect all of the plots. One of the more useful plot options is UNPACK. By default, all of the plots in a group are displayed together in a single panel (screen). If you specify UNPACK as an option on the PLOTS statement, each plot will appear in a separate screen (and each is therefore larger and easier to read).

It's time for an example. Suppose you want PROC TTEST to produce all plots for the two-sample *t*-test that was carried out in the previous example. In addition, you want each of the plots on a separate screen. You would write:

Program 6.3: Selecting Plots Using the PLOT Option for PROC TTEST

```
ods graphics on;
proc ttest data=example.blood_pressure
   plots(unpack shownull) = all;
   class Gender;
   var SBP DBP;
run;
ods graphics off;
```

In this example, you are telling PROC TTEST to unpack all of the plots. The keyword ALL is a request to produce all of the plots that are available with PROC TTEST.

The SHOWNULL option displays a vertical reference line at the null hypothesis value (zero by default) on the plot of mean differences. That plot shows the value of the difference between the sample means and the confidence interval (95% by default) around the value. If the confidence interval includes the null hypothesis value, the implication is that the difference is not statistically significant at your chosen alpha level (ALPHA=0.05 by default).

Because you have already seen most of the plots that are available for PROC TTEST, only the difference interval plot for SBP is shown. Notice the vertical line at zero. This line is displayed because Program 6.3 specifies the SHOWNULL option.

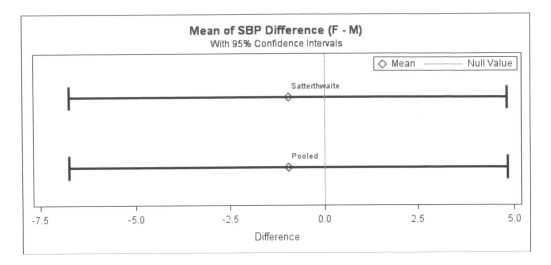

In this plot, both 95% confidence intervals include zero, which indicates that the mean difference in SBP values for males and females is not significantly different from zero.

Conducting a Paired *t*-test

If you have a design in which each subject received two treatments and you want to conduct a *t*-test, you need a PAIRED statement with PROC TTEST. As an example, a study was conducted to determine whether a reading program could improve the reading speed of eight subjects. The before and after reading speeds, along with a subject number, are stored in a SAS data set called `reading`. Here is a listing of this data set:

Listing of READING

Subj	Before	After
1	100	110
2	120	121
3	130	140
4	90	110
5	85	92
6	133	137
7	210	209
8	155	179

Program 6.4 shows how to request a paired *t*-test that compares the Before and After scores.

Program 6.4: Conducting a Paired *t*-test

```
title "Demonstrating a Paired T-test";
proc ttest data=reading;
   paired After*Before;
run;
```

The PAIRED statement tells the procedure that you have a paired design. The asterisk between the variable names on the PAIRED statement tells the procedure that you want to test the difference between these two variables. In this example, the difference is computed as After minus Before. Here is the output:

Demonstrating a Paired T-test

The TTEST Procedure

Difference: After - Before

N	Mean	Std Dev	Std Err	Minimum	Maximum
8	9.3750	8.7821	3.1049	-1.0000	24.0000

Mean	95% CL Mean		Std Dev	95% CL Std Dev	
9.3750	2.0330	16.7170	8.7821	5.8065	17.8739

DF	t Value	Pr > |t|
7	3.02	0.0194

You see that the reading program did indeed increase reading speeds (by an average of 9.375 words per minute), with a p-value of .0194.

You can specify several requests for a paired analysis by using a compact notation. An asterisk between two variable names tells SAS to conduct a paired *t*-test between the two variables (first value minus the second value). If you want to conduct paired *t*-tests on several variables, you can combine an asterisk and a colon to specify multiple tests. The following table was taken from the SAS online documentation. It shows how you use an asterisk and a colon to specify multiple paired *t*-tests in a compact notation.

PAIRED statement...	Resulting comparison(s)
PAIRED A*B;	A-B
PAIRED A*B C*D;	A-B and C-D
PAIRED (A B)*(C D);	A-C, A-D, B-C, and B-D
PAIRED (A B)*(C B);	A-C, A-B, and B-C
PAIRED (A1-A2)*(B1-B2);	A1-B1, A1-B2, A2-B1, and A2-B2
PAIRED (A1-A2):(B1-B2);	A1-B1 and A2-B2

With the PAIRED statement, an asterisk specifies a variable pair to test. You can list several pairs on a single PAIRED statement. Parentheses indicate that you want to request multiple paired tests—every variable in one set of parentheses versus every variable in the second set of parentheses. A colon between two lists instructs SAS to pair each variable in the first list with the corresponding variables in the second list.

Assumption Violations

The final example in this chapter demonstrates how the diagnostics produced by ODS Graphics can help you decide when the assumptions for a *t*-test have not been met.

In this example, you want to compare Income by Gender, using a SAS data set called salary. You might suspect that the distribution of Salary is not normal. The program and the Q-Q plots that follow make this clear.

Here is the program:

Program 6.5: Using ODS Plots to Test *t*-Test Assumptions

```
ods graphics on;
title "Comparing Income by Gender";
proc ttest data=salary;
   class Gender;
   var Income;
run;
ods graphics off;
```

The two diagnostic plots, which are generated by default, clearly show that the distribution of Income is not normal.

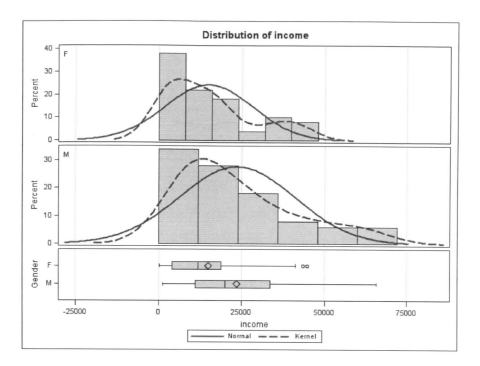

This plot shows that the Income distribution for both men and women is positively skewed.

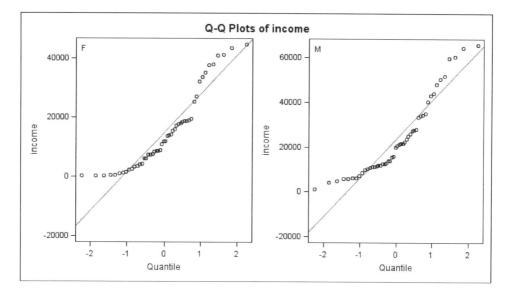

You can also see the deviation from normality in these Q-Q plots.

At this point, you might decide to use either a transformation to create values that are closer to normal, or a nonparametric test (see Chapter 12 for a description of nonparametric two-sample tests).

Conclusions

In this chapter, you learned how to use PROC TTEST to compare means between two groups for unpaired or paired data. In addition, you saw how to display plots from ODS Graphics and how to use the online help facility to obtain information about the plots that are available with each statistical procedure.

When you have more than two groups, multiple *t*-tests are not appropriate—instead, analysis of variance (ANOVA) is one of the more popular statistical tools. ANOVA is the topic of the next chapter.

Inferential Statistics – Comparing More than Two Means

Introduction

This chapter covers one- and two-way analysis of variance (ANOVA). ODS Statistical Graphics (referred to as ODS Graphics) generates a variety of plots that summarize your results. You also get plots that help you access the validity of the assumptions that must be met when you are running an analysis of variance.

A Simple One-way Design

The data set `store` contains the following variables:

Variable Name	Type	Description
Region	Character	Region of the country (North, East, South, West)
Advertising	Character	Advertising (Yes or No)
Gender	Character	Gender of shopper (M or F)
Book_Sales	Numeric	Amount spent on books
Music_Sales	Numeric	Amount spent on music
Electronics_Sales	Numeric	Amount spent on electronics
Total_Sales	Numeric	Total sales

Suppose you want to determine whether the mean of the variable Electronics_Sales varies by region of the country. You can use PROC GLM (general linear model) to conduct a one-way ANOVA. In addition, you can request summary and diagnostic plots using ODS Graphics. Here is the program:

Program 7.1: Running a One-Way ANOVA

```
ods graphics on;
title "Running a One-Way ANOVA Using PROC GLM";
proc glm data=store plots = diagnostics;
   class Region;
   model Electronics_Sales = Region / ss3;
   means Region / hovtest;
run;
quit;
ods graphics off;
```

You start by turning ODS Graphics on. Next, you tell PROC GLM that you want to use data from the `store` data set (`data=store`). If you do not include a PLOTS option with PROC GLM and you run a one-way design, ODS Graphics produces a default plot—a box plot that shows the distribution of Electronics_Sales for each Region. The option DIAGNOSTICS adds an additional panel of plots, as you will see in a moment.

You specify the independent variable on a CLASS statement. You use a MODEL statement to specify your dependent variable as well as your design. Following the keyword MODEL, you specify one or more dependent variables, followed by an equal sign. (An analysis is performed on each dependent variable that you list.) Following the equal sign, you specify your model. Because this example is a one-way design, you simply list the single independent variable.

By default, PROC GLM produces both a Type I and Type III sum of squares (SS) as output. For one-way designs, these will always be the same. For factorial designs, the Type I SS shows the effect of each factor as it is entered into the design; the type III SS shows the effect of each factor, controlling for all the other factors. You will probably want Type III sums of squares for your ANOVA designs. To avoid having SAS print both the Type I and Type III sums of squares, you can specify SS3 as an option on the MODEL statement. As a general rule, you specify statement options by entering them after a forward slash, as you did in Program 7.1.

The MEANS statement that follows the MODEL statement requests that PROC GLM print the mean and standard deviation for your dependent variable for each value of your independent variable. The HOVTEST option on the MEANS statement requests that SAS perform Levene's test for homogeneity of variance.

The order of statements within a procedure usually does not matter. However, in PROC GLM, you must specify your CLASS statement before your MODEL statement and your MODEL statement before the MEANS statement (or before other statements such as least square means or contrasts).

PROC GLM uses RUN-group processing. The procedure remains in memory so that you can submit additional models or modify previously executed models. The QUIT statement terminates the procedure. Don't worry if you forget the QUIT statement. SAS closes the procedure if you submit another PROC or DATA step.

Let's examine the output section-by-section:

Running a One-Way ANOVA Using PROC GLM ❶

The GLM Procedure

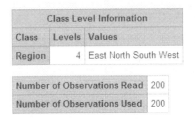

Class Level Information		
Class	Levels	Values
Region	4	East North South West

Number of Observations Read	200
Number of Observations Used	200

❶ The first part of the PROC GLM output tells you that Region has four levels (values), the number of observations read was 200, and the number of observations used was 200. This information is important. If there were any data errors for Region, the number of levels would include each unique value, including erroneous values, which would make your analysis invalid. If you have any missing values for any of your dependent or independent variables, those observations are not included in the analysis. When you run models with many independent variables, you might see that many observations were not used because one or more of these variables had missing values.

Running a One-Way ANOVA Using PROC GLM ❷

The GLM Procedure

Dependent Variable: Electronics_Sales

Source	DF	Sum of Squares	Mean Square	F Value	Pr > F
Model	3	329106.428	109702.143	20.82	<.0001
Error	196	1032773.072	5269.250		
Corrected Total	199	1361879.500			

R-Square	Coeff Var	Root MSE	Electronics_Sales Mean
0.241656	18.68218	72.58960	388.5500

Source	DF	Type III SS	Mean Square	F Value	Pr > F
Region	3	329106.4275	109702.1425	20.82	<.0001

❷ This portion of the output shows the analysis of variance table. You see the sources of variation (Model and Error), degrees of freedom, sum of squares, mean squares, the F-value, and the corresponding p-value. In this example, the F-value is 20.82. With 3 and 196 degrees of freedom, the p-value is less than .0001.

Further down in this output, you see the R-square (the proportion of variation in the dependent variable that is explained by the model), the coefficient of variation (the root mean square error, expressed as a percent of the mean), the root mean square error (the square root of the error variance), and the mean of the dependent variable.

At the very bottom of the output, you see an analysis of the independent variable (Region), which is identical to the information at the top of the listing. These identical values are to be expected because this test was a one-way ANOVA and the only explained portion of variation is due to the Region variable. Because the SS3 option is on the MODEL statement, this portion of the output shows the results for Type III SS only.

Running a One-Way ANOVA Using PROC GLM ❸

The GLM Procedure

Levene's Test for Homogeneity of Electronics_Sales Variance ANOVA of Squared Deviations from Group Means					
Source	DF	Sum of Squares	Mean Square	F Value	Pr > F
Region	3	78036410	26012137	0.59	0.6199
Error	196	8.5892E9	43822583		

❸ In this section, you see Levene's test for homogeneity of variance. This test is actually an analysis of variance that compares the squared deviations in each of the regions. With a p-value of .6199, you fail to reject the null hypothesis of equal variance. If this p-value were small, say, less than .05, you might consider some alternative methods of analyzing your data. However, you should keep in mind that analysis of variance is robust with regard to the assumption of homogeneity of variance, especially if you have a balanced design (an equal number of observations for each level of your independent variable). If you decide that the violation of this assumption is a problem, you can consider nonparametric alternatives to ANOVA (see Chapter 12) or you can use the WELCH option on the MEANS statement. This option gives weights to the cell means, based on the inverse of the variance (that is, groups with smaller variance are given more weight).

Running a One-Way ANOVA Using PROC GLM ❹

The GLM Procedure

Level of Region	N	Electronics_Sales	
		Mean	Std Dev
East	36	400.555556	72.7792924
North	69	364.782609	74.6483658
South	45	345.111111	64.4071644
West	50	451.800000	76.3902441

❹ This last section of output, generated by the MEANS statement, shows the mean and standard deviation for each Region.

You might want to look at the summary and diagnostic plots before going any further. Here is the diagnostic panel:

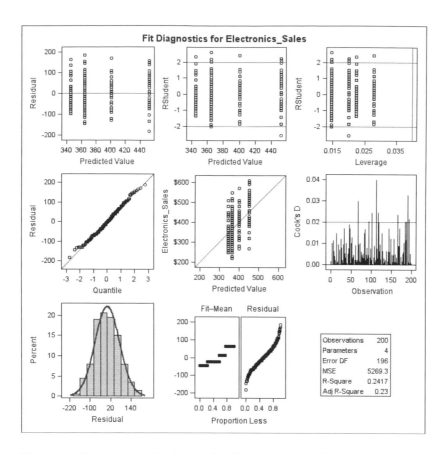

If you prefer to see each plot on the diagnostic panel on a separate page, you can specify the UNPACK option on the PLOTS request, like this:

```
plots(unpack) = diagnostics
```

The default diagnostic output contains nine plots. You can use options to control exactly which plots are produced, but it is probably not worth the effort—just ignore the plots that you don't care about.

If you imagine that the plots in the previous display are numbered from 1 to 9 (left to right, top to bottom), Plot 1 shows the residuals for each value of Region. This output gives you an idea of the variances within each region and is a nice addition to Levene's test.

Plot 2 shows similar information, except that the residuals are expressed as studentized residuals. These residuals are computed by dividing each residual by its standard error, where the standard error is computed with that data point removed from the calculation (sometimes called an externally studentized residual).

By examining the Q-Q plot in Plot 4 you can decide whether the residuals are normally distributed. Because the residuals in this plot fall mostly on the diagonal line, this assumption seems to be met.

Plot 7 (bottom left) is a histogram of residuals. This plot also confirms the assumption that they are normally distributed.

One of the default plots that is produced by PROC GLM is a box plot, which includes each level of the CLASS variable:

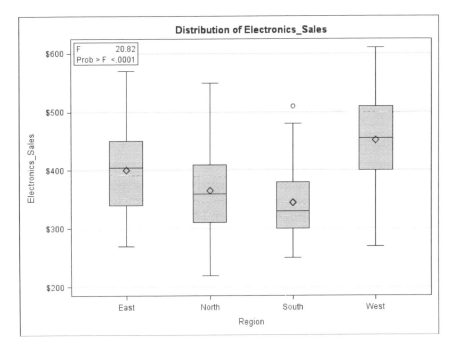

Here you see that sales of electronics seem to be higher in the west and lower in the south. To test all the pairwise comparisons, you need to include a request for multiple comparison tests on the MEANS statement. The next section explains this process.

Conducting Multiple Comparison Tests

You should probably consider the ANOVA results and multiple comparison tests only after you are satisfied that your test assumptions have been met. However, you will probably find it more convenient to request multiple comparisons when you run PROC GLM the first time. Then, if your model fails to meet the model assumptions, or if you do not obtain a significant result, you can ignore the results.

Some of the more popular multiple comparison tests are the Tukey and Student-Newman-Keuls (SNK) tests. You request either of these as options on the MEANS statement. For example, to request an SNK test, you use:

```
means Region / snk;
```

You can also specify an alpha level other than the default value of .05, like this:

```
means Region / snk alpha=.10;
```

Another way to test all possible pairwise comparisons is to specify the PDIFF option on the LSMEANS statement. The LSMEANS statement computes least square means. With a one-way design, the adjusted LSMEANS are the same as the values produced by the MEANS statement (however, the PDIFF option is not available on the MEANS statement). When you use the PDIFF option, you can also choose what method of Type I error adjustment you want to use. If you do not specify an adjustment method, the comparisons are made using the Tukey method. Popular adjustment options are TUKEY, BON (Bonferroni), and DUNNETT (Dunnett's test). You can get unadjusted pairwise tests by using the ADJUST=T option.

Program 7.2 shows how to request multiple comparisons using both of these methods:

Program 7.2: Requesting Multiple Comparison Tests

```
title "Requesting Multiple Comparison Tests";
proc glm data=store;
   class Region;
   model Electronics_Sales = Region / ss3;
   means Region / snk;
   lsmeans Region / pdiff adjust=tukey;
run;
quit;
```

Notice that `adjust=tukey` was included as an option even though the Tukey adjustment is the default if you do not request an adjustment method. This option is included so that it is clear to anyone who reads this program that a Tukey adjustment is being used—some people might not realize that Tukey is the default adjustment.

PROC GLM uses an interesting method to display all the possible pairwise comparisons. Take a look at the following portion of the output:

Requesting Multiple Comparison Tests

The GLM Procedure

Student-Newman-Keuls Test for Electronics_Sales

Note: This test controls the Type I experimentwise error rate under the complete null hypothesis but not under partial null hypotheses.

Alpha	0.05
Error Degrees of Freedom	196
Error Mean Square	5269.25
Harmonic Mean of Cell Sizes	47.34134

Note: Cell sizes are not equal.

Number of Means	2	3	4
Critical Range	29.424369	35.235947	38.660845

Means with the same letter are not significantly different.			
SNK Grouping	Mean	N	Region
A	451.80	50	West
B	400.56	36	East
C	364.78	69	North
C			
C	345.11	45	South

The means are listed from largest to smallest. In the column labeled SNK Grouping, any two means with the same grouping letter are not significantly different at the .05 level. In this example, the sales for the West region are significantly different from the others. Sales for the East region are also significantly different from all the other regions. Because the sales for the North and South regions both have the same grouping letter (C), sales in these regions are not significantly different from each other. You might be wondering why a letter C appears in the blank row between the North and South values. SAS places a 'C' here so that it is easy to see that North and South form a non-significant pair.

The PDIFF option on the LSMEANS statement gives you the actual p-value between every pair of means. Here is that portion of the output:

Requesting Multiple Comparison Tests

The GLM Procedure
Least Squares Means
Adjustment for Multiple Comparisons: Tukey-Kramer

Region	Electronics_Sales LSMEAN	LSMEAN Number
East	400.555556	1
North	364.782609	2
South	345.111111	3
West	451.800000	4

Least Squares Means for effect Region Pr > |t| for H0: LSMean(i)=LSMean(j) Dependent Variable: Electronics_Sales			
i/j	1	2	3	4
1		0.0810	0.0043	0.0079
2	0.0810		0.4919	<.0001
3	0.0043	0.4919		<.0001
4	0.0079	<.0001	<.0001	

In this output, each of the means is listed (in alphabetical order by Region) and given a number from 1 to 4 (labeled LSMEAN Number). Below this section is a matrix that shows the p-value between all possible pairs of means. For example, the p-value between 1 and 2 (East and North) is .0810; the p-value between 1 and 3 (East and South) is .0043, and so forth. Because you specified ADJUST=Tukey, these multiple comparisons are adjusted accordingly.

Using ODS Graphics to Produce a Diffogram

ODS Graphics can produce a diffogram (also known as a means-means plot) as a visual way of exploring the pairwise differences. Program 7.3 shows how to request this plot:

Program 7.3: Using ODS Graphics to Produce a Diffogram

```
ods graphics on;
title "Requesting Multiple Comparison Tests";
proc glm data=store plots(only) = diffplot;
   class Region;
   model Electronics_Sales = Region / ss3;
   means Region / snk;
   lsmeans Region / pdiff adjust=tukey;
run;
quit;
ods graphics off;
```

If you want to see only the diffogram and not the other plots that PROC GLM produces by default, include the ONLY option on the plot request. The ONLY option instructs SAS to produce only the plots that you are requesting and not to produce the other default plots. The keyword DIFFPLOT requests the diffogram. The output from this program is identical to that produced by Program 7.2, so this discussion includes only the diffogram:

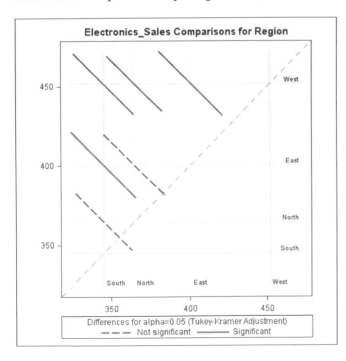

The four regions are listed on the x- and y-axes to form a matrix. At the intersection of any two regions, you see the difference between them. The solid or dashed diagonal lines at the intersection of any two regions represent the 95% CI on the difference score for those two regions. The main, positively sloping diagonal line on the diffogram represents a difference of zero. If any of the confidence intervals cross this main diagonal, those two means are not significantly different. To help you distinguish the outcomes, the lines that represent significant differences are solid and the lines that represent non-significant differences are displayed as dashes.

Two-way Factorial Designs

To demonstrate a two-way factorial design, you can test for electronics sales by Region and Gender. To specify this design on the MODEL statement, you have two choices:

```
model Electronics_Sales = Region Gender Region*Gender;

model Electronics_Sales = Region | Gender;
```

In the first method, the asterisk specifies an interaction between Region and Gender; in the second method, the vertical bar between Region and Gender specifies a factorial design. The second notation is convenient when your models have many factors and you do not want to write all the high-order interaction terms.

If your model does have several factors, you can place a limit on the interaction terms with a convenient notation. For example, if you specify a three-way factorial design (like Region, Gender, and Advertising) and you do not want any interactions higher than second order, you would write:

```
model Electronics_Sales = Region | Gender | Advertising @2;
```

The @2 at the end of the statement is an instruction to limit the interaction terms to second order.

Using the vertical bar notation, you can specify a factorial model with Region and Gender as independent variables, like this:

Program 7.4: Performing a Two-Way Factorial Design

```
title "Performing a Two-way Factorial design";
proc glm data=store;
   class Region Gender;
   model Electronics_Sales = Region | Gender / ss3;
   lsmeans Region | Gender;
run;
quit;
```

The first portion of the output is shown next:

Performing a Two-way Factorial design ❶

The GLM Procedure

Dependent Variable: Electronics_Sales

Source	DF	Sum of Squares	Mean Square	F Value	Pr > F
Model	7	533841.480	76263.069	17.68	<.0001
Error	192	828038.020	4312.698		
Corrected Total	199	1361879.500			

R-Square	Coeff Var	Root MSE	Electronics_Sales Mean
0.391989	16.90159	65.67114	388.5500

Source	DF	Type III SS	Mean Square	F Value	Pr > F
Region	3	331827.2810	110609.0937	25.65	<.0001
Gender	1	196917.0078	196917.0078	45.66	<.0001
Region*Gender	3	10422.6951	3474.2317	0.81	0.4922

❶ You can see that both Region and Gender are significant ($p < .0001$), but the interaction between Region and Gender is not significant.

Performing a Two-way Factorial design ❷

The GLM Procedure
Least Squares Means
Adjustment for Multiple Comparisons: Tukey-Kramer

Region	Electronics_Sales LSMEAN	LSMEAN Number
East	410.844156	1
North	368.615385	2
South	345.642292	3
West	453.028846	4

Least Squares Means for effect Region Pr > |t| for H0: LSMean(i)=LSMean(j) Dependent Variable: Electronics_Sales				
i/j	1	2	3	4
1		0.0131	0.0001	0.0219
2	0.0131		0.2675	<.0001
3	0.0001	0.2675		<.0001
4	0.0219	<.0001	<.0001	

❷ The next portion of the output shows the adjusted means for Region and the Tukey adjusted pairwise comparisons for Region.

Performing a Two-way Factorial design ❸

The GLM Procedure
Least Squares Means
Adjustment for Multiple Comparisons: Tukey-Kramer

Gender	Electronics_Sales LSMEAN	H0:LSMean1=LSMean2 Pr > |t|
Female	361.955762	<.0001
Male	427.109578	

❸ Here you see the adjusted means for Gender and the comparison of Female and Male (because Gender has only two levels, you can use the p-value from the ANOVA table).

Performing a Two-way Factorial design ❹

The GLM Procedure
Least Squares Means
Adjustment for Multiple Comparisons: Tukey-Kramer

Region	Gender	Electronics_Sales LSMEAN	LSMEAN Number
East	Female	364.545455	1
East	Male	457.142857	2
North	Female	339.230769	3
North	Male	398.000000	4
South	Female	321.739130	5
South	Male	369.545455	6
West	Female	422.307692	7
West	Male	483.750000	8

Least Squares Means for effect Region*Gender Pr > |t| for H0: LSMean(i)=LSMean(j) Dependent Variable: Electronics_Sales								
i/j	1	2	3	4	5	6	7	8
1		0.0014	0.8346	0.6108	0.3650	1.0000	0.0541	<.0001
2	0.0014		<.0001	0.1056	<.0001	0.0033	0.7497	0.9297
3	0.8346	<.0001		0.0071	0.9720	0.6669	<.0001	<.0001
4	0.6108	0.1056	0.0071		0.0011	0.7827	0.8647	<.0001
5	0.3650	<.0001	0.9720	0.0011		0.2279	<.0001	<.0001
6	1.0000	0.0033	0.6669	0.7827	0.2279		0.1079	<.0001
7	0.0541	0.7497	<.0001	0.8647	<.0001	0.1079		0.0246
8	<.0001	0.9297	<.0001	<.0001	<.0001	<.0001	0.0246	

❹ In this final section, you see the mean electronics sales for each combination of Region and Gender. Because the interaction between Region and Gender is not significant, you are probably not interested in comparing these cell means. For example, if you compared Region=East, Gender=Female to Region=West, Gender=Female, you would get .0541.

Analyzing Factorial Models with Significant Interactions

This section demonstrates how to analyze a two-way factorial design when there is a significant interaction. The `store` data set was created so that there is an interaction between Region and Gender for the variable Music_Sales. The program to analyze this model is identical to Program 7.4, but the variable Music_Sales is substituted for Electronics_Sales:

Program 7.5: **Analyzing a Factorial Design with Significant Interactions**

```
title "Analyzing a Factorial Design with a Significant Interaction";
ods graphics on;
proc glm data=store;
   class Region Gender;
   model Music_Sales = Region | Gender / ss3;
   lsmeans Region | Gender / pdiff adjust=tukey;
run;
quit;
ods graphics off;
```

The following portion of the output shows the main effects and the interaction term:

Analyzing a Factorial Design with a Significant Interaction

The GLM Procedure

Dependent Variable: Music_Sales

Source	DF	Sum of Squares	Mean Square	F Value	Pr > F
Model	7	21195.35081	3027.90726	17.96	<.0001
Error	192	32364.14919	168.56328		
Corrected Total	199	53559.50000			

R-Square	Coeff Var	Root MSE	Music_Sales Mean
0.395735	17.20768	12.98319	75.45000

Source	DF	Type III SS	Mean Square	F Value	Pr > F
Gender	1	7170.48161	7170.48161	42.54	<.0001
Region	3	13139.46726	4379.82242	25.98	<.0001
Region*Gender	3	4507.82347	1502.60782	8.91	<.0001

Because the interaction of Region and Gender is significant (p < .0001) you cannot easily interpret the main effects. Before you embark on the next step, the interaction plot created by ODS Graphics will shed some light on why the interaction is significant.

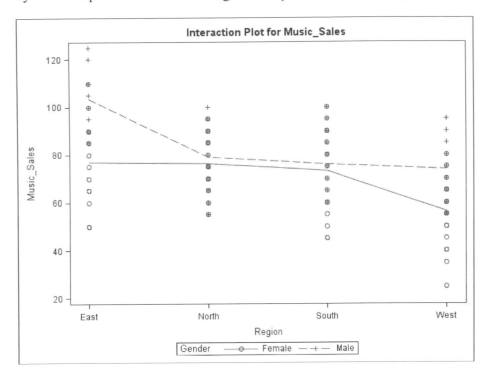

In this plot, you see that the Region by Gender interaction is mostly the result of higher sales for males in the east and lower sales for females in the west.

One way to make comparisons between specific regions and genders is to examine the LSMEANS matrix. However, SAS provides a powerful tool that you can use to compare Gender for each Region. You can make such a comparison by specifying a SLICE option on the LSMEANS statement. For this problem, you could use the following LSMEANS statement:

```
lsmeans Region*Gender / slice=Region;
```

This statement results in the following output:

Analyzing Factorial Design with a Significant Interaction

The GLM Procedure
Least Squares Means

Region*Gender Effect Sliced by Region for Music_Sales					
Region	DF	Sum of Squares	Mean Square	F Value	Pr > F
East	1	6019.922439	6019.922439	35.71	<.0001
North	1	125.261984	125.261984	0.74	0.3897
South	1	92.974308	92.974308	0.55	0.4586
West	1	3871.157051	3871.157051	22.97	<.0001

Here you see a comparison of Gender for each Region. From this analysis, you can see significant gender differences in the East and West regions.

Analyzing a Randomized Block Design

You can specify a randomized block design using a MODEL statement that is similar to the one in the previous factorial design—you just need to omit the interaction term. For example, if you want to compare Book_Sales by Gender, and you also want to control for Region, you can write:

Program 7.6: Analyzing a Randomized Block Design

```
title "Analyzing a Randomized Block Design";
proc glm data=store;
   class Region Gender;
   model Book_Sales = Gender Region / ss3;
   lsmeans Gender;
run;
quit;
```

In this model, you are treating Region as a blocking factor and assuming that there is no interaction between the blocking factor and the predictor of interest, Gender. The following displays show portions of the output:

Source	DF	Type III SS	Mean Square	F Value	Pr > F
Gender	1	36291.16711	36291.16711	13.33	0.0003
Region	3	11933.57335	3977.85778	1.46	0.2266

Analyzing a Randomized Block Design

The GLM Procedure
Least Squares Means

Gender	Book_Sales LSMEAN
Female	287.903474
Male	260.754290

In this output, you see that Gender is significant (p=.0003), and you see the adjusted means.

Conclusions

In this chapter, you learned how to run analysis of variance models, starting from simple one-way designs and ending with *n*-way factorial designs with interactions. You saw that by using ODS Graphics you can quite easily test the assumptions for conducting these analyses. Finally, you learned how to perform a variety of multiple comparison tests to investigate pairwise differences.

In the next chapter, you will learn how to investigate relationships between two continuous variables and how to run simple linear regression.

Correlation and Regression

Introduction

In this chapter, you will learn how to compute correlation coefficients (both parametric and nonparametric) and how to run simple linear regression models. With the introduction of ODS Statistical Graphics (referred to as ODS Graphics), you can generate correlation matrix scatter plots. With this same facility, you can test assumptions that are required for linear and multiple regression. Let's get started.

Producing Pearson Correlations

You can use PROC CORR to compute correlations between every variable in one list against every variable in another list or to create a correlation matrix. When teamed up with ODS Graphics, PROC CORR can automatically produce individual scatter plots or a matrix of scatter plots.

The data set exercise contains the following variables:

Variable Name	Description
Subj	Subject number
Age	Age of subject
Pushups	Maximum number of push-ups
Rest_Pulse	Resting pulse rate
Max_Pulse	Maximum pulse rate
Run_Pulse	Pulse rate while running

Suppose you want to see the correlations between Pushups and the variables Age, Rest_Pulse, Max_Pulse, and Run_Pulse. The following program computes these correlations and produces scatter plots that correspond to each of the variable pairs:

Program 8.1: Producing Correlations between Two Sets of Variables

```
ods graphics on;
title "Computing Pearson Correlation Coefficients";
proc corr data=exercise nosimple rank;
   var Rest_Pulse Max_Pulse Run_Pulse Age;
   with Pushups;
run;
ods graphics off;
```

When you specify a VAR and a WITH statement, you generate Pearson correlations between every variable in the VAR list with every variable in the WITH list. Program 8.1 uses two options, NOSIMPLE and RANK. The NOSIMPLE option tells the procedure that you do not want the default output of means and standard deviations for each of the variables in the VAR and WITH lists. The RANK option says to order the correlations from largest to smallest (by their absolute values). In this example, ODS Graphics is turned on. Here are the results:

Computing Pearson Correlation Coefficients

The CORR Procedure

1 With Variables:	Pushups
4 Variables:	Rest_Pulse Max_Pulse Run_Pulse Age

Pearson Correlation Coefficients, N = 50 Prob > |r| under H0: Rho=0				
Pushups	Rest_Pulse	Age	Max_Pulse	Run_Pulse
	-0.49639	-0.49191	-0.45010	-0.34555
	0.0002	0.0003	0.0010	0.0140

The output shows the correlation of Pushups with each of the other variables. In the table, the first number in each column is the Pearson correlation coefficient, and the second number is the p-value for a test of the null hypothesis that the population coefficient (rho) is equal to 0. In this example, 50 observations make up each correlation. If there were missing values and each pair of variables had a different *n*, the sample size would have been listed along with each correlation. In this example, each of the correlations was significant with a p-value less than .05.

ODS Graphics produces the following panel:

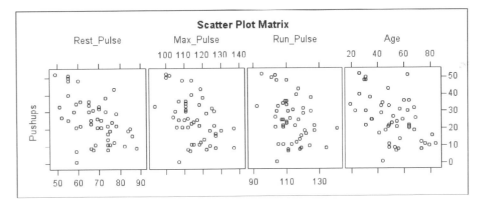

Two types of plots are available when you use ODS Graphics with PROC CORR, a panel or matrix of scatter plots (as the one above) or individual scatter plots. By default (if you do not include a PLOTS= option), you get a panel of scatter plots. Because ODS plots a maximum of five variables in a panel, you need to override this default limit if you want to see more variables. To include more variables in your panel (up to a maximum of ten), you can use the NVAR=ALL or NVAR=*n* option on the request, like this:

```
proc corr data=exercise nosimple rank plots = matrix(nvar=all);
```

In Chapter 4, you learned that you can use PROC SGSCATTER to display a scatter plot matrix, with no limitation on the number of variables displayed (except for a practical limit, after which the plots become too small).

If you want to see each scatter plot on a separate page, you can include a PLOTS= option, like this:

```
proc corr data=exercise nosimple rank plots(only)=scatter;
```

The ONLY option says that you want only separate bivariate plots for each variable pair, rather than the scatter plot matrix that is produced by default. By default, the maximum number of individual plots is also set at five. You can use the same NVAR= option to request additional scatter plots as you used with the matrix plot. The maximum number of individual scatter plots is 10. (Again, you can use PROC SGSCATTER to produce any number of plots.)

The following example shows an individual scatter plot of Pushups by Rest_Pulse:

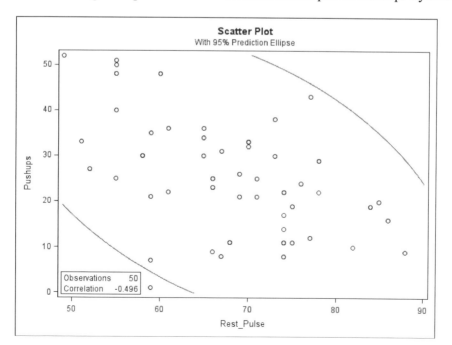

Notice that SAS has drawn a 95% prediction ellipse. You can eliminate the ellipse by specifying the option ELLIPSE=NONE, like this:

```
proc corr data=exercise nosimple rank
   plots(only) = scatter(ellipse = none);
```

Generating a Correlation Matrix

If you list all of your variables on a VAR statement with PROC CORR (omitting the WITH statement), SAS produces a correlation matrix—the correlation of every variable with every other variable. If you also include an ODS GRAPHICS ON statement, the procedure produces a matrix of scatter plots—really cool. Here is an example, using all the variables from the `exercise` data set:

Program 8.2: Producing a Correlation Matrix

```
ods graphics on;
title "Computing Pearson Correlation Coefficients";
proc corr data=exercise nosimple
   plots = matrix(histogram);
   var Pushups Rest_Pulse Max_Pulse Run_Pulse Age;
run;
ods graphics off;
```

The PLOTS= option is included so that you can include the HISTOGRAM option. Without this option, the diagonal of the scatter plot matrix would contain variable names. By specifying this option, you get a histogram of each of the variables on the diagonal (see the correlation matrix that follows the output listing).

The following display shows the tabular and graphic output:

Computing Pearson Correlation Coefficients

The CORR Procedure

5 Variables:	Pushups Rest_Pulse Max_Pulse Run_Pulse Age

Pearson Correlation Coefficients, N = 50 Prob > |r| under H0: Rho=0					
	Pushups	**Rest_Pulse**	**Max_Pulse**	**Run_Pulse**	**Age**
Pushups	1.00000	-0.49639	-0.45010	-0.34555	-0.49191
		0.0002	0.0010	0.0140	0.0003
Rest_Pulse	-0.49639	1.00000	0.83112	0.76139	0.48774
	0.0002		<.0001	<.0001	0.0003
Max_Pulse	-0.45010	0.83112	1.00000	0.93634	0.26582
	0.0010	<.0001		<.0001	0.0621
Run_Pulse	-0.34555	0.76139	0.93634	1.00000	0.25097
	0.0140	<.0001	<.0001		0.0788
Age	-0.49191	0.48774	0.26582	0.25097	1.00000
	0.0003	0.0003	0.0621	0.0788	

This listing shows the correlation of every variable with every other variable, along with the associated p-values. And here is the scatter plot matrix that is produced by ODS Graphics:

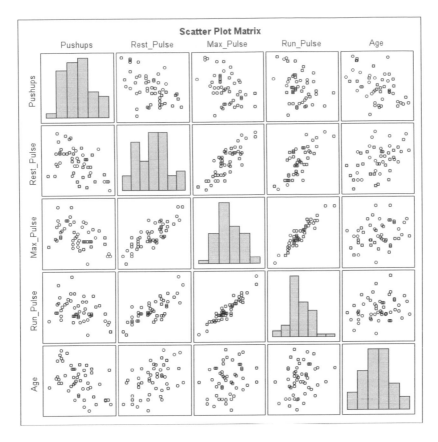

Here you see a scatter plot of every variable with every other variable, and histograms of each variable plotted on the diagonal.

Creating HTML Output with Data Tips

When you create HTML output using ODS Statistical Graphics, you can add the capability of placing the mouse pointer on a point and having SAS display information about that point (such as the value of the ID variable identifying the point). SAS calls this capability "Data Tips." To activate this facility, use the command:

```
ods graphics / imagemap = on;
```

Consider the following program, which produces scatter plots:

Program 8.3: Creating HTML Output That Contains Data Tips

```
ods graphics on / imagemap=on; ❶
ods listing close; ❷

ods html gpath='c:\books\statistics by example' ❸
         path='c:\books\statistics by example'
         file='scatter.html'
         style=statistical;
title "Computing Pearson Correlation Coefficients";
proc corr data=exercise nosimple
plots(only)=scatter(ellipse=none); ❹
   var Rest_Pulse Max_Pulse Run_Pulse Age;
   with Pushups;
   id Subj; ❺
run;
ods html close; ❻
ods graphics off;
ods listing;
```

❶ First, you need to use the IMAGEMAP=ON option on the ODS GRAPHICS statement. ❷ Next, because you want only HTML output and not the normal listing, you close the listing output.

❸ This statement sets up the destinations for the HTML and graphics output. Although you can supply the entire path for the HTML output using the FILE= option, it is easier to use a separate PATH= option to identify the folder where you want the HTML files to go. When you use PATH=, you only need to supply a filename (using the FILE= option) for your HTML file. In this example, an HTML file called **scatter.html** is being put into a folder called **c:\books\statistics by example**. SAS automatically gives names to each piece of graphics output and those files will be placed in the folder you named on the GPATH= option.

❹ In this program, a PLOTS= option requests scatter plots (one for each of the VAR variables versus Pushups). ❺ An ID statement specifies Subj as the ID variable. In this way, the data tips facility will be able to identify a subject number when you point to a data point on one of the scatter plots. ❻ Finally, the HTML and graphics locations are closed and the listing is turned back on.

The next scatter plot demonstrates how data tips work. The cursor was placed on a data point and information about that data point popped up.

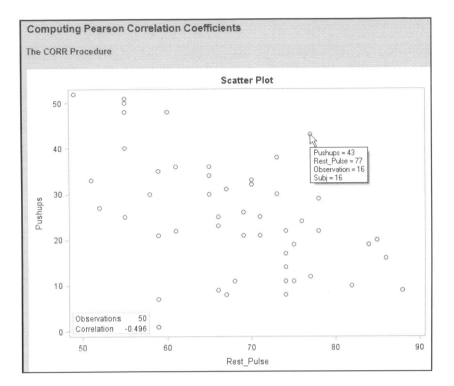

Generating Spearman Nonparametric Correlations

PROC CORR can also produce Spearman rank correlations. Just supply the option SPEARMAN on the PROC CORR statement, and the procedure computes Spearman coefficients. When you include this option, SAS does not produce Pearson coefficients. If you want both Spearman and Pearson correlations, you need to specify both the SPEARMAN and PEARSON options. As an example, here is Program 8.1, modified to compute Spearman correlations:

Program 8.4: Generating Spearman Rank Correlations

```
title "Computing Spearman Rank Correlations";
proc corr data=exercise nosimple spearman;
   var Rest_Pulse Max_Pulse Run_Pulse Age;
   with Pushups;
run;
```

The following output shows the resulting correlations and p-values:

Computing Spearman Rank Correlations

The CORR Procedure

1 With Variables:	Pushups
4 Variables:	Rest_Pulse Max_Pulse Run_Pulse Age

Spearman Correlation Coefficients, N = 50 Prob > |r| under H0: Rho=0				
	Rest_Pulse	Max_Pulse	Run_Pulse	Age
Pushups	-0.48882	-0.45181	-0.33960	-0.46625
	0.0003	0.0010	0.0158	0.0006

You will sometimes find it useful to produce both Spearman and Pearson correlations and take note of those variable pairs for which the two correlations differ substantially.

Running a Simple Linear Regression Model

Suppose you want to predict how many push-ups a person can do, based on his or her resting pulse (which is the variable that has the strongest correlation with Pushups). You can use PROC REG to run both simple and multiple regression models. This procedure also contains a variety of variable selection methods as well as a comprehensive set of diagnostic tools.

You will see how to run multiple regression models in the next chapter. For now, let's run a simple linear regression model:

Program 8.5: Running a Simple Linear Regression Model

```
ods graphics on;
title "Running a Simple Linear Regression Model";
proc reg data=exercise;
   model Pushups = Rest_Pulse;
run;
quit;
ods graphics off;
```

Notice that this procedure uses a QUIT statement. This procedure supports RUN-group processing, as does PROC GLM and several other procedures. Remember that RUN-group processing means that the procedure remains in memory and enables you to run several different models (each followed by a RUN statement) without having to submit another PROC REG statement.

In this program, you have also turned on ODS Graphics (without a PLOTS= option, so that it produces a series of default plots). Here is the output:

Running a Simple Linear Regression Model

The REG Procedure
Model: MODEL1
Dependent Variable: Pushups

Number of Observations Read	50 ❶
Number of Observations Used	50

Analysis of Variance ❷					
Source	DF	Sum of Squares	Mean Square	F Value	Pr > F
Model	1	1958.50151	1958.50151	15.69	0.0002
Error	48	5989.99849	124.79164		
Corrected Total	49	7948.50000			

Root MSE	11.17102	R-Square	0.2464	❸
Dependent Mean	25.30000	Adj R-Sq	0.2307	
Coeff Var	44.15422			

Parameter Estimates ❹					
Variable	DF	Parameter Estimate	Standard Error	t Value	Pr > |t|
Intercept	1	69.48749	11.26531	6.17	<.0001
Rest_Pulse	1	-0.65077	0.16427	-3.96	0.0002

❶ The first part of the output shows the number of observations read and the number of operations that were used to calculate the results. This section is important. If you have missing values for the dependent or independent variable, those observations are not included in the analysis. This fact becomes even more important for multiple regression because you can have a large number of predictor variables. In that case, if any of the predictor variables has a missing value, the entire observation is not included in the analysis.

❷ Here you see the standard analysis of variance table, showing the sources of variation, degrees of freedom, sum of squares, mean squares, F-value, and p-value. In this example

with only one predictor variable, you reject the null hypothesis that the slope is zero
(p < .0002).

❸ Further down, you see the root MSE, the R-square and adjusted R-square. The root
MSE is the square root of the mean square error (124.79) from the ANOVA table. This
number represents the variation in the system due to error (derived from the deviations of
each data point to the regression line) in standard deviation units. R-square, also called
the coefficient of determination, represents the proportion of variability in the dependent
variable that can be explained by the regression model. The adjusted R-square adjusts for
the number of predictor (independent) variables in the model and is of interest when you
are running multiple regression models (a topic that is covered in the next chapter).

In this same section, you see the dependent mean and the coefficient of variation. The
dependent mean is the mean of your dependent variable. In this example, the mean
number of push-ups is 25.3. Finally, the value labeled Coeff Var (often written as CV) is
the coefficient of variation. This number (22.15) is the standard deviation of the error
(root MSE) expressed as a percentage of the mean. In this example, root MSE is about
44% of the mean. Because this is a unitless measure, you can use this number to compare
the error between models in which the units of the dependent variable are different.

❹ This section shows you the parameter estimates, along with their standard errors and
t- and p-values. In this simple regression model, the value of the intercept is the value of
the dependent variable when the resting pulse is zero. Because a pulse rate of zero for
someone in this experiment would be unusual (and cause for great alarm), there is no
valid interpretation of the intercept value. Also, testing this value against the null
hypothesis that it is zero is not meaningful either.

The parameter for Rest_Pulse is the coefficient of the resting pulse term in the model (the
beta). Interestingly, there is a small probability (p=.0002) that this value came from a
population in which this parameter was zero (the baseline model).

In this example, the least squares regression equation for this model is:

```
Pushups = 69.48749 - .65077 * Rest_Pulse
```

The next part of the output that you will want to examine are the plots produced by ODS
Graphics.

The first panel contains diagnostic plots for the regression:

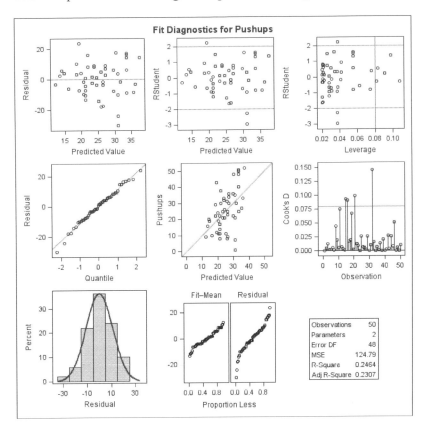

Here you can see the residuals expressed as raw values or standardized as Studentized residuals. Also of interest are the Q-Q plots and histograms of the residuals. Finally, a plot of Cook's D will give you some idea of influential points (more on this later). In the next program, you will see how to override the default plots and produce individual plots that will help you identify influential observations.

Two other plots are produced by default. The following plot shows the residuals versus the resting pulse values. In this example, the residuals appear to be randomly distributed about 0. You should be looking for several things in this plot. First, if the points show a systematic deviation about the zero line, you might need to add more terms to your model (possibly a non-linear term). Also, you should look at the deviations about 0 for different values of the dependent variable. You might see, for example, an increase or a decrease in the variability, with increasing values of the dependent variable. This outcome would be a violation of the assumption that the standard deviation of the residuals was the same for each value of the independent variable.

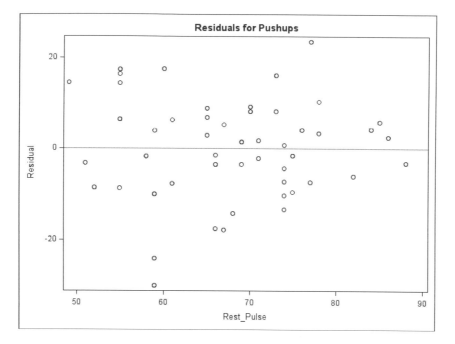

The last plot shows the original data points, the regression line, and two confidence limits (one for the mean of the dependent variable and one showing the confidence limits for individual data points). It is important to understand the difference in these two confidence limits. The shaded, inner band is a confidence limit on the mean value of the dependent variable. That is, given an x-value, you are 95% confident that the mean of y is within this band. The outer, wider band indicated by the dashed lines is the 95% confidence interval for individual points; given an x-value, you are 95% confident that any individual y-value will be within this region. Here is the plot:

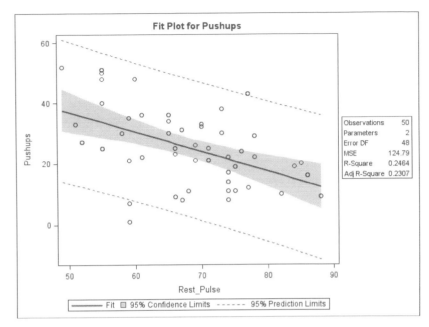

Using ODS Statistical Graphics to Investigate Influential Observations

SAS provides several measures to help you identify influential data points—points that have more than their fair share of influence on the fitted line or surface. Almost all of these measures use the same concept: run the regression model with and without a given observation and see the effect on the predicted value or on the betas. Depending on the nature of your data, you need to decide what to do after you have identified influential observations. In general, you can't just remove them. Some of the influential points might be the result of data errors. If that is the case, you need to correct the errors and rerun the analysis. You might want to investigate exactly why certain points are influential and, perhaps, gain some insight into your data. Finally, if you do decide to remove data points, you need to indicate that you have done so and provide a rationale for this decision.

Program 8.6 is the same as Program 8.5, but with the INFLUENCE and R (residual) options added on the MODEL statement. These options cause SAS to produce some commonly used influence statistics. You can also add a PLOTS= option with PROC REG to obtain plots that show influential observations. (If you also add an ID statement and use a LABEL option for the plots, SAS identifies influential points on the plots, using values of the ID variable.)

Program 8.6: Displaying Influential Observations

```
ods graphics on;
ods listing close;
title "Displaying Influential Observations";
proc reg data=exercise plots(only) = (cooksd(label)
    rstudentbypredicted(label));
    id Subj;
    model Pushups = Rest_Pulse / influence r;
run;
quit;
ods graphics off;
ods listing;
```

The INFLUENCE option gives you statistics that show you how much each observation changes aspects of the regression depending on whether that observation is included. The R option gives you more details about the residuals, as well as the value of the Cook's D statistic.

Here is a portion of the output (the first few observations) that shows what you get when you use the INFLUENCE and R options:

Displaying Influential Observations

The REG Procedure
Model: MODEL1
Dependent Variable: Pushups ❶

			Output Statistics					
Obs	Subj	Dependent Variable	Predicted Value	Std Error Mean Predict	Residual	Std Error Residual	Student Residual
1	1	19.0000	20.6795	1.9637	-1.6795	10.997	-0.153
2	2	36.0000	29.7903	1.9444	6.2097	11.001	0.564
3	3	11.0000	21.3303	1.8708	-10.3303	11.013	-0.938
4	4	35.0000	31.0919	2.1525	3.9081	10.962	0.357
5	5	24.0000	20.0287	2.0655	3.9713	10.978	0.362
6	6	14.0000	21.3303	1.8708	-7.3303	11.013	-0.666
7	7	21.0000	24.5841	1.5901	-3.5841	11.057	-0.324

❶ The first few columns of the output show the subject identifier (Subj), the value of the dependent variable, the predicted value of this variable, and the standard error of the predicted value. In addition, you see the residual, the standard error of the residual, and the residual expressed as a Studentized value (the residual divided by the standard error of the residual).

❷ -2-1 0 1 2	Cook's D	RStudent	Hat Diag H	Cov Ratio	❸ DFFITS	DFBETAS Intercept	DFBETAS Rest_Pulse
I I I	0.000	-0.1512	0.0309	1.0752	-0.0270	0.0128	-0.0160
I I* I	0.005	0.5604	0.0303	1.0614	0.0991	0.0685	-0.0577
I *I I	0.013	-0.9368	0.0280	1.0341	-0.1591	0.0655	-0.0852
I I I	0.002	0.3533	0.0371	1.0775	0.0694	0.0538	-0.0471
I I I	0.002	0.3584	0.0342	1.0740	0.0674	-0.0358	0.0434
I *I I	0.006	-0.6617	0.0280	1.0534	-0.1124	0.0463	-0.0602
I I I	0.001	-0.3211	0.0203	1.0599	-0.0462	-0.0012	-0.0052
I I*** I	0.044	1.6260	0.0335	0.9673	0.3027	0.2230	-0.1921

❷ This next portion shows the Studentized residuals in a graphical display. This information is displayed far better in the ODS Statistical Graphics plots that you will see shortly. The column labeled RStudent is a variation (and, in this author's opinion, a great refinement) on the Studentized residuals that were included in the previous table. SAS computes the RStudent value by computing the residual between each data point and a regression line that was computed with that data point removed, and then dividing by the standard error. Why is this computation necessary? If you have a very influential data point, it will pull the line (or surface) closer to the point. Then, when you compute the residual, you get a smaller value than if you had computed the regression with the data point omitted. Various texts refer to the RStudent residuals as deleted residuals or externally standardized residuals.

Cook's D measures the effect of each data point on the predicted value. The ODS Graphics plot is a better way to see which data points have large values for this statistic.

❸ Let's look at the column labeled DFFITS (difference in fit statistics). This value reflects an overall change in the betas (slopes) if you run the regression with and without each data point.

The last two columns of the output are of interest only when you are running multiple regression models. The DFBETAS (difference in the betas) show the effect of the data point in question on each of the betas in your model. The DFBETAS are discussed in the next chapter.

The PLOTS= option requests two plots: one showing Cook's D, and the other showing Studentized residuals by predicted values. The LABEL option places values of the ID variable (Subj in this program) on the plot to identify data points that exceed the standard cutoff for Cook's D (4/n, where n is the number of observations), or it puts points on the Studentized residual plot that exceed plus or minus 2. Here are the two plots:

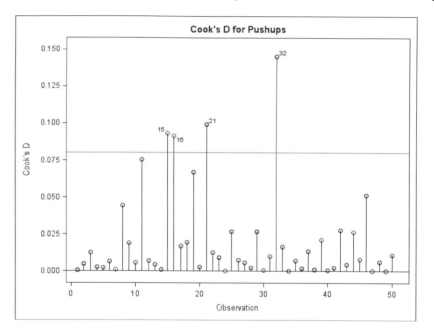

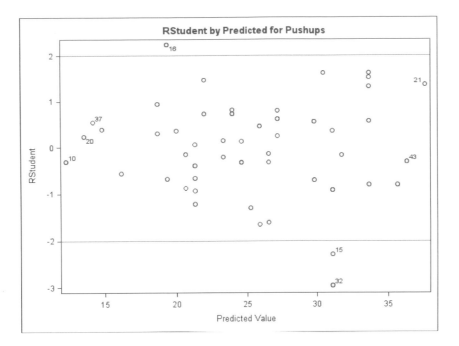

The labels that you see on the data points that exceed the cutoff values are the subject numbers (variable Subj) for those data points. Also labeled are data points with very high or low values of the predicted value (points 10, 22, 37, 43, and 21).

Using the Regression Equation to Do Prediction

Now that you have a least squares regression equation, you can use this equation to predict values of the dependent variable. You can use several approaches to accomplish this.

Because you know the intercept and the betas from the model, you can simply compute the value of the dependent variable with a calculator (or with your phone if it has that capability). However, that method is not elegant. After all, you are using a computer, aren't you?

If you want SAS to do the calculations, the simplest way is to create a data set that contains the values of the independent variable for which you want to predict the value of the dependent variable. If you create such a data set, you can add these observations to the original data set that you used to run the regression. Because the added observations have missing values for the dependent variable, they will not affect the regression computation. The following program demonstrates this approach.

Program 8.7: Predicting Values Using the Regression Equation

```
data need_predictions;
   input Rest_Pulse @@;
datalines;
50 60 70 80 90
;
data combined;
   set exercise need_predictions;
run;
```

The data set `need_predictions` contains five observations with values for Rest_Pulse. The double trailing at signs (@@) on the INPUT statement let you create several observations from one line of data. SAS usually goes to a new line for each iteration of the DATA step. The double trailing at signs are an instruction to "hold the line" and not skip to the next record when the DATA step iterates.

Also notice the DATALINES statement. When you use this statement you can place your data lines directly in the program and avoid the trouble of creating a separate external text file and then writing an INFILE statement to tell SAS where to find the data. For those readers old enough to remember, this statement used to be called CARDS (as in computer punch cards—if you have no idea what this refers to, Google it and see how we did things in the old days).

To concatenate the observations from the original data set (`exercise`) and the newly created data set (`need_predictions`), you use a SET statement. This statement causes all the observations to be read from the `exercise` data set and the five new observations to be added to the bottom. To be sure this whole concept is clear, here are the last eight observations from the resulting data set, `combined`:

Last 8 Observations from Data Set COMBINED

Obs	Subj	Age	Pushups	Rest_Pulse	Max_Pulse	Run_Pulse
48	48	46	19	84	130	127
49	49	31	22	74	118	108
50	50	79	10	82	124	124
51	.	.	.	50	.	.
52	.	.	.	60	.	.
53	.	.	.	70	.	.
54	.	.	.	80	.	.
55	.	.	.	90	.	.

If you run your regression model with this combined data set and use the P (predicted) option on the MODEL statement, you will get the predicted values for these five values of Rest_Pulse. Here is the program:

Program 8.8: Using PROC REG to Compute Predicted Values

```
title "Using PROC REG to Compute Predicted Values";
proc reg data=combined;
   model Pushups = Rest_Pulse / p;
   id Rest_Pulse;
run;
quit;
```

The P option on the MODEL statement prints the predicted value for each observation. The ID statement adds the variable Rest_Pulse to the output. Before you look at the part of the output that shows you the predicted values, take note of the following section:

Using PROC REG to Compute Predicted Values

The REG Procedure
Model: MODEL1
Dependent Variable: Pushups

Number of Observations Read	55
Number of Observations Used	50
Number of Observations with Missing Values	5

Notice that the number of observations read is now 55 (the original 50 plus the 5 observations from the `need_predictions` data set). However, only 50 observations are used in the regression because the additional 5 observations have missing values for the variable Pushups.

Now here's the portion of the output where you see the predicted values:

Using PROC REG to Compute Predicted Values

The REG Procedure
Model: MODEL1
Dependent Variable: Pushups

		Output Statistics		
Obs	Rest_Pulse	Dependent Variable	Predicted Value	Residual
1	75	19.0000	20.6795	-1.6795
2	61	36.0000	29.7903	6.2097
3	74	11.0000	21.3303	-10.3303

46	55	48.0000	33.6950	14.3050
47	71	25.0000	23.2826	1.7174
48	84	19.0000	14.8226	4.1774
49	74	22.0000	21.3303	0.6697
50	82	10.0000	16.1241	-6.1241
51	50	.	36.9488	.
52	60	.	30.4411	.
53	70	.	23.9334	.
54	80	.	17.4256	.
55	90	.	10.9179	.

Remember that the column showing the values of Rest_Pulse is present as a result of the ID statement in the program.

A More Efficient Way to Compute Predicted Values

The process just described might be OK for small data sets, but is highly inefficient when you have large data sets (especially when there are many independent variables). The efficient and elegant way to compute predicted values is to run the regression on the original data and write the model parameters to a data set. You can then use PROC SCORE to take these regression parameters and compute predicted values for new values of the independent variable:

Program 8.9: Describing a More Efficient Way to Compute Predicted Values

```
title "Describing a More Efficient Way to Compute Predicted Values";
proc reg data=exercise noprint outest=betas;
    model Pushups = Rest_Pulse;
run;
quit;
proc print data=betas noobs;
run;
```

The NOPRINT option tells the procedure that you do not want any printed output. The OUTEST= (output estimates) option tells PROC REG that you want the regression parameters to be written to a data set (that is called `betas`). To see exactly what is happening, here is what the data set `betas` looks like:

Describing a More Efficient Way to Compute Predicted Values

MODEL	_TYPE_	_DEPVAR_	_RMSE_	Intercept	Rest_Pulse	Pushups
MODEL1	PARMS	Pushups	11.1710	69.4875	-0.65077	-1

This data set has only one observation (there would be more if you ran several models). The variable called Intercept is the y-intercept (beta 0) for the model, and the variable Rest_Pulse is the beta for slope. The _TYPE_ variable, which is equal to PARMS, will be important later when you use PROC SCORE to compute predicted values (this procedure can use several types of data to compute scores such as factor scores, and it uses the _TYPE_ value to know what type of data it is dealing with).

So, to finish up the prediction, you need to run PROC SCORE, like this:

Program 8.10: Using PROC SCORE to Compute Predicted Values from a Regression Model

```
proc score data=need_predictions score=betas
    out=predictions type=parms;
    var Rest_Pulse;
run;

title "Using PROC SCORE to Compute Predicted Values";
proc print data=predictions noobs;
run;
```

The data set `need_predictions` is the one that was created by Program 8.7. It contains five observations with values for Rest_Pulse; these observations are the ones for which you want predictions for the number of push-ups a person can do. The SCORE= option tells PROC SCORE the name of the data set that contains the regression parameters, and OUT= names the data set that will contain the predicted values. Note that this procedure creates only data sets—it does not create printed output.

The VAR statement specifies which variables to use to make the prediction (Rest_Pulse in this example). Next, PROC PRINT lists the observations that are in data set `predictions`:

Using PROC SCORE to Compute Predicted Values

Rest_Pulse	MODEL1
50	36.9488
60	30.4411
70	23.9334
80	17.4256
90	10.9179

This output shows the predicted number of push-ups a person can do, given his or her resting pulse rate.

Conclusions

In this chapter, you learned how to produce individual scatter plots as well as a scatter plot matrix. You learned that you can use PROC SGPLOT and PROC SGSCATTER to produce these plots, or you can use ODS Statistical Graphics along with PROC CORR to compute the correlations and generate the plots at the same time.

In addition to computing Pearson correlations, you learned that you can also compute Spearman nonparametric correlations using PROC CORR. Finally, you learned how to use PROC REG to run simple linear regression models, and how to interpret ODS Graphics associated with this procedure, to test the underlying assumptions required for this analysis.

In the next chapter, you will use PROC REG to perform multiple regression. You will see several methods that you can use to select models for prediction or to help explain relationships among your variables.

Multiple Regression

Introduction

This chapter covers multiple regression models. You will learn how to generate diagnostics to help select variables for a model as well as how to perform stepwise techniques. The same diagnostics that are available with simple linear regression can be used with multiple regression models. When you have multiple predictor variables in a model, you will also need tests for collinearity.

Multiple regression involves trying to predict a dependent variable by looking at multiple independent variables. This process is complex, both statistically and conceptually. It is almost always wise to develop a model of how you think the independent variables should be related to the dependent variables before going too far with any analysis. It is easy to be led astray by relying too much on the computer.

Fitting Multiple Regression Models

Let's start by using the same `exercise` data set from the previous chapter. As a reminder, here is the content of this data set:

Variable Name	Description
Subj	Subject number
Age	Age of subject
Pushups	Maximum number of push-ups
Rest_Pulse	Resting pulse rate
Max_Pulse	Maximum pulse rate
Run_Pulse	Pulse rate while running

Program 9.1 is a fixed model that uses Age and Max_Pulse to predict how many push-ups a person can do (Pushups variable).

Program 9.1: Running a Multiple Regression Model

```
title "Running a Multiple Regression Model";
proc reg data=exercise;
   model Pushups = Age Max_Pulse;
run;
quit;
```

The syntax is straightforward—you name your dependent (outcome) variable, followed by an equal sign, followed by as many predictor (independent) variables as you want in your model. PROC REG computes an intercept and a coefficient (beta) for each of these predictor variables. Here is the output:

Running a Multiple Regression Model

The REG Procedure
Model: MODEL1
Dependent Variable: Pushups

Number of Observations Read	50
Number of Observations Used	50

Analysis of Variance ❶					
Source	DF	Sum of Squares	Mean Square	F Value	Pr > F
Model	2	2795.54147	1397.77074	12.75	<.0001
Error	47	5152.95853	109.63742		
Corrected Total	49	7948.50000			

Root MSE	10.47079	R-Square	0.3517	❷
Dependent Mean	25.30000	Adj R-Sq	0.3241	
Coeff Var	41.38652			

Parameter Estimates ❸					
Variable	DF	Parameter Estimate	Standard Error	t Value	Pr > |t|
Intercept	1	96.65502	18.89988	5.11	<.0001
Age	1	-0.31605	0.09613	-3.29	0.0019
Max_Pulse	1	-0.47750	0.16929	-2.82	0.0070

❶ The analysis of variance table shows that you should reject the null hypothesis that all the betas (except for the intercept) are zero.

❷ The R-square will increase as you add predictor variables to the model, so the adjusted value is more useful when you are comparing models.

❸ You see here that both Age and Max_Pulse are significant (p=.0019 and .0070 respectively).

Running All Possible Regressions with *n* Variables

A useful way to decide which set of predictor variables generates your best model is to use a selection method called RSQUARE. If you have *n* predictor variables, this selection method runs all possible models with each variable alone, then with all variables taken two at a time, three at a time, etc. For *n* predictor variables, this process generates 2^n-1 possible models. In the example that follows, four predictor variables result in 16-1=15 models.

The next program demonstrates the RSQUARE selection method:

Program 9.2: Using the RSQUARE Selection Method to Execute All Possible Models

```
ods graphics on;
title "Demonstrating the RSQUARE Selection Method";
proc reg data=exercise;
   model Pushups = Age Rest_Pulse Max_Pulse Run_Pulse /
   selection = rsquare cp adjrsq;
run;
quit;
ods graphics off;
```

You use the MODEL option SELECTION=RSQUARE to instruct the procedure to run all possible regression models. Two additional options, CP (Mallows' C_p), and ADJRSQ (adjusted R-square) are included. The adjusted R-square value takes the number of predictor variables into account and is useful in comparing models with different numbers of predictor variables. Mallows' C_p helps you decide if you have too few or too many predictor variables in your model. Two decision rules that use C_p are discussed later in this chapter. Here is the output:

Demonstrating the RSQUARE Selection Method

The REG Procedure
Model: MODEL1
Dependent Variable: Pushups

R-Square Selection Method

| Number of Observations Read | 50 |
| Number of Observations Used | 50 |

Number in Model	R-Square	Adjusted R-Square	C(p)	Variables in Model
1	0.2464	0.2307	10.4785	Rest_Pulse
1	0.2420	0.2262	10.8103	Age
1	0.2026	0.1860	13.7615	Max_Pulse
1	0.1194	0.1011	19.9961	Run_Pulse
2	0.3517	0.3241	4.5862	Age Max_Pulse
2	0.3283	0.2997	6.3423	Age Rest_Pulse
2	0.2946	0.2646	8.8650	Age Run_Pulse
2	0.2510	0.2191	12.1369	Rest_Pulse Max_Pulse
2	0.2493	0.2174	12.2591	Max_Pulse Run_Pulse
2	0.2489	0.2169	12.2914	Rest_Pulse Run_Pulse
3	0.3995	0.3603	3.0068	Age Max_Pulse Run_Pulse
3	0.3527	0.3105	6.5096	Age Rest_Pulse Max_Pulse
3	0.3284	0.2846	8.3329	Age Rest_Pulse Run_Pulse
3	0.2901	0.2439	11.1998	Rest_Pulse Max_Pulse Run_Pulse
4	0.3996	0.3462	5.0000	Age Rest_Pulse Max_Pulse Run_Pulse

For all models that have one variable, two variables, etc., you see the R-square values, listed from highest to lowest. The adjusted R-squares and C_p are also listed.

When you have a large number of predictor variables, you can limit the number of models that are listed in the output by using the MODEL option BEST=*n*. You will see a demonstration of this option in the next section. Note that although this option limits the number of models printed in the output, all possible regressions are still computed.

ODS Statistical Graphics (referred to as ODS Graphics) produced two panels (by default, because the PLOTS= option was not included on the procedure). The first is a diagnostics panel:

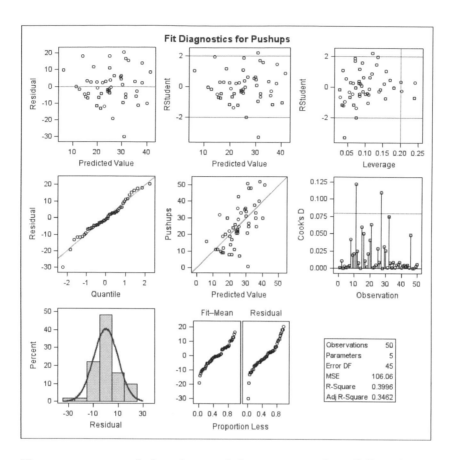

Here you see several plots that can help you assess the validity of the regression assumptions. These plots are generated from the model that contains all four of the predictor variables. These diagnostic plots are the same ones that are produced when you run simple linear regression and that are described in the previous chapter. The second panel shows more plots involving residuals:

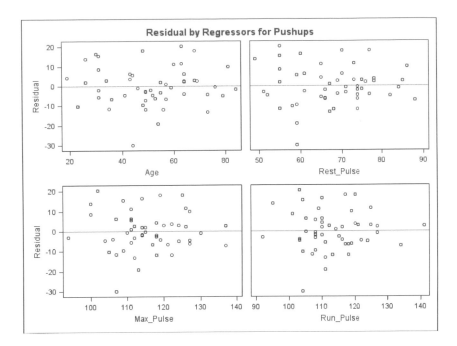

Here you see the residuals plotted against each of the predictor variables. There does not appear to be any systematic pattern to these plots, and the variability of the residuals across values of the predictor variables does not seem to show a pattern—two desirable results.

Producing Separate Plots Instead of a Panel

Program 9.2 produced two panels, one showing fit diagnostics and the other showing residuals by regressors. If you prefer each of the plots in both panels to be displayed on a separate plot, you need to add a PLOTS= option, specify the two panels you want, and use the UNPACK option, as follows:

```
plots(unpack) = (diagnostics residualplot)
```

DIAGNOSTICS and RESIDUALPLOT are the names of the two default plots that are produced when you run PROC REG with ODS Graphics turned on. You can obtain the names of these two plots from SAS Help (select SAS Products → SAS Procedures → PROC REG → ODS Graphics). You can also obtain the plot names from the Results window of the Display Manager. Place the cursor on one of the plots and right-click to see the plot properties.

Because the UNPACK option is on the left-hand side of the equal sign, it applies to all the plots that you requested. What if you want some plots to be unpacked and others to be on a single panel? In this case, you place the UNPACK option after each of the plot names that you want unpacked. For example, to see each plot on the diagnostic panel separately and the residual plots on a single panel, you would use:

```
plots = (diagnostics(unpack) residualplot)
```

Choosing the Best Model (C_p and Hocking's Criteria)

You can use Mallows' C_p to help you decide which model is best. If your model has too few variables, you might benefit from adding additional variables; if your model has too many variables, you might have overspecified the model.

Beginning with the simplest model, Mallows suggested that you choose the first model in which C_p is less than or equal to p, where p is the number of parameters (predictor variables plus the intercept) in the model. Hocking proposed an additional selection criterion for selecting models. He suggested that you use Mallows' criteria if you are using the regression to make predictions and an alternative criterion if you are using the regression to explain relationships among the predictors and the dependent variable. For the second purpose, Hocking recommended that you choose the first model where C_p is less than or equal to $2p - p_{full} + 1$, where p_{full} is the number of parameters in a full model (a model that uses all of the predictor variables). ODS Graphics includes plots that show you the best model based on both of these two criteria.

To see plots of C_p, R-square, and adjusted R-square, add a PLOTS= option on PROC REG, like this:

Program 9.3: Generating Plots of R-Square, Adjusted R-Square, and C_p

```
ods graphics on;
title "Generating Plots of R-Square, Adjusted R-Square and C(p)";
proc reg data=exercise plots(only) = (rsquare adjrsq cp);
   model Pushups = Age Rest_Pulse Max_Pulse Run_Pulse /
   selection = rsquare cp adjrsq;
run;
quit;
ods graphics off;
```

The keyword ONLY on the PLOTS request is an instruction to produce only the plots requested and not to include all the plots that are produced by default.

Now let's look at the three plots.

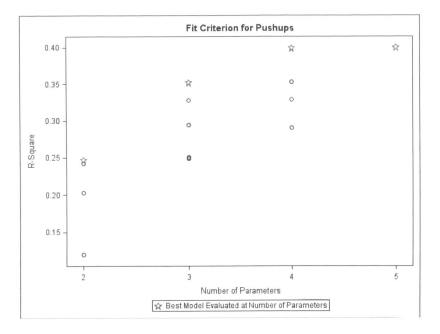

This plot shows the R-square value versus the number of parameters. Adding variables to a model always increases the R-square value. Therefore, the full model always has the largest R-square. The model with the largest R-square value for each of the models is starred.

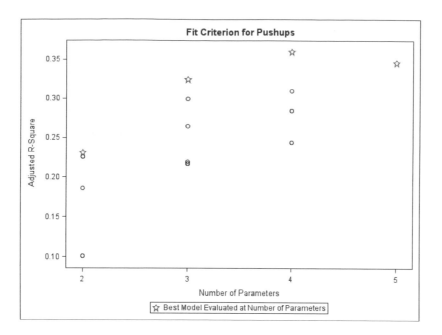

This plot shows the adjusted R-square values for each of the models. Adjusted R-square provides a fairer comparison of the different models than R-square does.

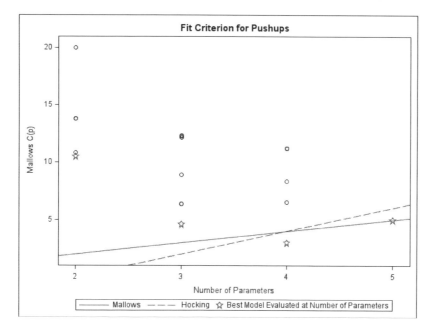

This last plot shows Mallows' C_p for each of the models. Two lines that represent Mallows' criteria and Hocking's criteria are also included. Using these lines, it is easy to see that the model that best fulfills Mallows' and Hocking's criteria has four parameters (which is a 3-variable model). In many cases, the model that you select using Mallow's criterion will be the more parsimonious model, that is, the simpler model with fewer parameters.

The models that these two criteria suggest are just that—suggestions. You should use your subject-matter expertise to make final decisions on which models you ultimately use.

If you have models with a large number of predictor variables, there might be some very high values of C_p, making it hard to see the part of the graph near the two lines. You can use the BEST=*n* MODEL option to limit the number of possible models for a given number of parameters, which makes the graph easier to read.

For example, you could limit your output to three models for each group of models by writing:

```
model Pushups = Age Rest_Pulse Max_Pulse Run_Pulse /
    selection = rsquare cp adjrsq best=3;
```

Forward, Backward, and Stepwise Selection Methods

When you have a large number of possible predictor variables, the processing time to run all possible models using the RSQUARE selection method can become excessive. In these situations, you can use one of the automatic selection methods—forward, backward, or stepwise.

To run any of these automatic selection methods, use the SELECTION= option on the PROC REG statement. The forward method starts with the single best variable (the one that yields the largest F statistic) and adds variables one at a time until the p-value for the variable being entered is larger than a specified value. The backward elimination method starts with all the variables in the model and removes them one at a time (the one with the largest p-value leaves first) until all variables being considered for removal have p-values smaller than a given value. Finally, the stepwise selection method is almost the same as the forward method except that a variable that has already been added to the model at a previous step might be removed later.

Two options, SLENTRY= (significance level for entering) and SLSTAY= (significance level for staying), have a default value for each of the three methods:

Method	Default Value
Forward	SLENTRY=.50
Backward	SLSTAY=.10
Stepwise	SLENTRY=.15, SLSTAY=.15

Program 9.4 demonstrates all three methods.

Program 9.4: Demonstrating Forward, Backward, and Stepwise Selection Methods

```
title "Forward, Backward, and Stepwise Selection Methods";
title2 "Using Default Values for SLENTRY and SLSTAY";
proc reg data=exercise;
  Forward: model Pushups = Age Rest_Pulse Max_Pulse Run_Pulse /
    selection = forward;
  Backward: model Pushups = Age Rest_Pulse Max_Pulse Run_Pulse /
    selection = backward;
  Stepwise: model Pushups = Age Rest_Pulse Max_Pulse Run_Pulse /
    selection = stepwise;
run;
quit;
```

This program demonstrates all three automatic selection methods: forward, backward, and stepwise. You can supply a label for each of the models by preceding the MODEL statement with the label, followed by a colon. In this program, the labels Forward, Backward, and Stepwise, are used. Because the labels are included in the output, adding these labels helps you identify which sections of output belong to which model.

Because there is a lot of output, only selected sections are presented. The excerpted portion of the output that is included shows the order in which the forward selection method selected variables.

Forward Selection Output

Forward, Backward, and Stepwise Selection Methods
Using Default Values for SLENTRY and SLSTAY

The REG Procedure
Model: Forward
Dependent Variable: Pushups

Number of Observations Read	50
Number of Observations Used	50

Forward Selection: Step 1

Variable Rest_Pulse Entered: R-Square = 0.2464 and C(p) = 10.4785 **❶**

Analysis of Variance					
Source	DF	Sum of Squares	Mean Square	F Value	Pr > F
Model	1	1958.50151	1958.50151	15.69	0.0002
Error	48	5989.99849	124.79164		
Corrected Total	49	7948.50000			

Variable	Parameter Estimate	Standard Error	Type II SS	F Value	Pr > F
Intercept	69.48749	11.26531	4748.01733	38.05	<.0001 **❷**
Rest_Pulse	-0.65077	0.16427	1958.50151	15.69	0.0002

Forward Selection: Step 2

Variable Age Entered: R-Square = 0.3283 and C(p) = 6.3423 **❸**

Variable	Parameter Estimate	Standard Error	Type II SS	F Value	Pr > F
Intercept	68.53895	10.75560	4613.00469	40.61	<.0001 **❹**
Age	-0.25862	0.10805	650.80083	5.73	0.0207
Rest_Pulse	-0.44118	0.17953	685.98528	6.04	0.0177

Forward Selection: Step 3

Variable Max_Pulse Entered: R-Square = 0.3527 and C(p) = 6.5096 **❺**

Variable	Parameter Estimate	Standard Error	Type II SS	F Value	Pr > F
Intercept	93.75861	21.90646	2048.76231	18.32	<.0001 **❻**
Age	-0.30104	0.11194	808.92824	7.23	0.0099
Rest_Pulse	-0.08690	0.32243	8.12382	0.07	0.7887
Max_Pulse	-0.40798	0.30948	194.36295	1.74	0.1939

Forward Selection: Step 4

Variable Run_Pulse Entered: R-Square = 0.3996 and C(p) = 5.0000 **❼**

Variable	Parameter Estimate	Standard Error	Type II SS	F Value	Pr > F
Intercept	93.56536	21.33252	2040.27798	19.24	<.0001 **❽**
Age	-0.31264	0.10918	869.64928	8.20	0.0063
Rest_Pulse	-0.02608	0.31565	0.72377	0.01	0.9345
Max_Pulse	-1.26238	0.54665	565.59846	5.33	0.0256
Run_Pulse	0.84388	0.45045	372.22539	3.51	0.0675

All variables have been entered into the model.

			Summary of Forward Selection **❾**				
Step	Variable Entered	Number Vars In	Partial R-Square	Model R-Square	C(p)	F Value	Pr > F
1	Rest_Pulse	1	0.2464	0.2464	10.4785	15.69	0.0002
2	Age	2	0.0819	0.3283	6.3423	5.73	0.0207
3	Max_Pulse	3	0.0245	0.3527	6.5096	1.74	0.1939
4	Run_Pulse	4	0.0468	0.3996	5.0000	3.51	0.0675

❶ The first variable entered is Rest_Pulse. ❷ The p-value for this variable is <.0001 (we are not really interested in the intercept). ❸ Age is entered next. ❹ The p-values for Age and Rest_Pulse are shown in this section. Notice that the p-value for Rest_Pulse has changed—the p-values always represent the contribution to each variable after all the other variables have been accounted for. ❺ In Step 3, Max_Pulse is entered. ❻ Notice that the p-value for Rest_Pulse is now greater than the default entry value of .50. In the forward method, after variables are entered, they are not removed. The most likely reason that the p-value for Rest_Pulse is so high is that is it highly correlated with Max_Pulse (we will discuss collinearity in a later section). ❼ The last variable to enter is Run_Pulse. ❽ This also causes all the p-values to change.

❾ After all the variables have been entered, a summary of the regression is shown. Besides the model R-square, this summary shows the partial R-square—the incremental change in R-square as each variable is entered.

Backward Selection Output

Forward, Backward, and Stepwise Selection Methods
Using Default Values for SLENTRY and SLSTAY

The REG Procedure
Model: Backward
Dependent Variable: Pushups

Number of Observations Read	50
Number of Observations Used	50

Backward Elimination: Step 0

All Variables Entered: R-Square = 0.3996 and C(p) = 5.0000 **①**

Analysis of Variance **②**					
Source	DF	Sum of Squares	Mean Square	F Value	Pr > F
Model	4	3175.89068	793.97267	7.49	0.0001
Error	45	4772.60932	106.05798		
Corrected Total	49	7948.50000			

Variable	Parameter Estimate	Standard Error	Type II SS	F Value	Pr > F	
Intercept	93.56536	21.33252	2040.27798	19.24	<.0001	**③**
Age	-0.31264	0.10918	869.64928	8.20	0.0063	
Rest_Pulse	-0.02608	0.31565	0.72377	0.01	0.9345	
Max_Pulse	-1.26238	0.54665	565.59846	5.33	0.0256	
Run_Pulse	0.84388	0.45045	372.22539	3.51	0.0675	

Backward Elimination: Step 1

Variable Rest_Pulse Removed: R-Square = 0.3995 and C(p) = 3.0068 **❹**

Variable	Parameter Estimate	Standard Error	Type II SS	F Value	Pr > F
Intercept	94.42444	18.42397	2725.62506	26.27	<.0001
Age	-0.31715	0.09352	1193.39331	11.50	0.0014
Max_Pulse	-1.28690	0.45409	833.41926	8.03	0.0068
Run_Pulse	0.84771	0.44320	379.62544	3.66	0.0620

All variables left in the model are significant at the 0.1000 level.

	Summary of Backward Elimination						
Step	Variable Removed	Number Vars In	Partial R-Square	Model R-Square	C(p)	F Value	Pr > F
1	Rest_Pulse	3	0.0001	0.3995	3.0068	0.01	0.9345

The backward elimination method starts with all the variables in the model. **❶** The R-square for the full model is .3996. **❷** The ANOVA table shows a significant model, with p <.0001. **❸** The p-values for each of the variables are listed. **❹** The first and only variable that is removed is Rest_Pulse.

Stepwise Selection Output

Forward, Backward, and Stepwise Selection Methods
Using Default Values for SLENTRY and SLSTAY

The REG Procedure
Model: Stepwise
Dependent Variable: Pushups

Number of Observations Read	50
Number of Observations Used	50

Stepwise Selection: Step 1

Variable Rest_Pulse Entered: R-Square = 0.2464 and C(p) = 10.4785 **❶**

Analysis of Variance					
Source	DF	Sum of Squares	Mean Square	F Value	Pr > F
Model	1	1958.50151	1958.50151	15.69	0.0002
Error	48	5989.99849	124.79164		
Corrected Total	49	7948.50000			

Variable	Parameter Estimate	Standard Error	Type II SS	F Value	Pr > F
Intercept	69.48749	11.26531	4748.01733	38.05	<.0001
Rest_Pulse	-0.65077	0.16427	1958.50151	15.69	0.0002

Stepwise Selection: Step 2

Variable Age Entered: R-Square = 0.3283 and C(p) = 6.3423 ❷

Variable	Parameter Estimate	Standard Error	Type II SS	F Value	Pr > F
Intercept	68.53895	10.75560	4613.00469	40.61	<.0001
Age	-0.25862	0.10805	650.80083	5.73	0.0207
Rest_Pulse	-0.44110	0.17953	685.98528	6.04	0.0177

All variables left in the model are significant at the 0.1500 level.

No other variable met the 0.1500 significance level for entry into the model.

Summary of Stepwise Selection ❸								
Step	Variable Entered	Variable Removed	Number Vars In	Partial R-Square	Model R-Square	C(p)	F Value	Pr > F
1	Rest_Pulse		1	0.2464	0.2464	10.4785	15.69	0.0002
2	Age		2	0.0819	0.3283	6.3423	5.73	0.0207

❶ In the stepwise model, Rest_Pulse is entered first. ❷ In Step 2, Age is entered. No other variables met the entry criteria of p < .15. ❸ The summary tables shows the R-square and partial R-square for each term.

Summary of the Three Models

Selection Method	Variables in the Final Model
Forward	Rest_Pulse, Age, Max_Pulse, Run_Pulse
Backward	Age, Max_Pulse, Run_Pulse
Stepwise	Rest_Pulse, Age

The main differences in these three models probably results from the vastly different entry or staying significance levels. To demonstrate this, the next program shows how to set the SLENTRY= option to .15 for the forward selection method:

Program 9.5: Setting the SLENTRY Value to .15 Using the Forward Selection Method

```
title "Forward Selection Method";
title2 "SLENTRY Set at .15";
proc reg data=exercise;
  Forward: model Pushups = Age Rest_Pulse Max_Pulse Run_Pulse /
    selection = forward slentry=.15;
run;
quit;
```

When you run this model, the variables that are selected are the same as the one you obtain using the stepwise method.

Forcing Selected Variables into a Model

Sometimes you want to use an automatic selection method like the stepwise method, but you also want to force one or more variables into the model. You can do this with an INCLUDE=*n* option on the MODEL statement. As an example, suppose that you want to run a stepwise model, and you also want to be sure that Max_Pulse is included in the model. You do this by placing Max_Pulse first in the list of predictor variables and adding INCLUDE=1 as a MODEL option. Here is the code:

Program 9.6: Forcing Variables into a Stepwise Model

```
title "Forcing Variables into a Stepwise Model";
proc reg data=exercise;
  model Pushups = Max_Pulse Age Rest_Pulse Run_Pulse /
    selection = stepwise include=1;
run;
quit;
```

When you run this model, Max_Pulse is forced to be entered first.

Creating Dummy (Design) Variables for Regression

Because regression models can include categorical variables, you might need to create dummy variables (also called design variables) that correspond to the values of a categorical variable. For example, suppose you want to predict Music_Sales (from the store data set) given Total_Sales, Gender, and Region. Gender has the values Male and Female, Region has the values North, East, South, and West. If a categorical variable has *k* levels, you need *k*–1 dummy variables. If you choose Male as the reference for Gender and West as the reference level for Region, you could write the following program:

Program 9.7: Creating Dummy Variables for Regression

```
data Dummy;
  set Store;
  *Create dummy variable for Gender;
  if Gender = 'Male' then Male = 1;
  else if Gender = 'Female' then Male = 0;
  *Create Dummy Variable for Region;
  if Region not in ('North' 'East' 'South' 'West') then
    call missing(North, East, South);
  else if Region = 'North' then North = 1;
  else North = 0;
  if Region = 'East' then East = 1;
  else East = 0;
  if Region = 'South' then South = 1;
  else South = 0;
run;
title "Creating and Using Dummy variables";
proc print data=Dummy(obs=10) noobs;
  var Region Gender Male North East South;
run;
```

As with all SAS programs, you need to be careful with missing or invalid values. In this program, if the value of Gender is Male, the dummy variable Male is set to 1. If the value of Gender is Female, the value of Male is set to 0. If Gender has a missing or invalid value, Male will be a missing value.

The next section of code creates three dummy variables for Region. You first test to be sure that Region has a valid, nonmissing value by using the IN operator. If Region is not equal to one of the values in the list that follows this operator, the CALL MISSING routine sets each of the three dummy variables to a missing value.

In this example, the three dummy variables North, East, and South are all numeric variables. In general, the CALL MISSING routine can set both character and numeric variables to a missing value.

When Region is equal to North, the dummy variable (North) is set to 1. Otherwise, it is set to 0. The two other dummy variables (East and South) are created in a similar manner.

To be sure the program works correctly, PROC PRINT lists the first ten observations.

Creating and Using Dummy variables

Region	Gender	Male	North	East	South
West	Male	1	0	0	0
West	Male	1	0	0	0
West	Female	0	0	0	0
South	Female	0	0	0	1
West	Female	0	0	0	0
West	Female	0	0	0	0
West	Male	1	0	0	0
North	Female	0	1	0	0
North	Male	1	1	0	0
North	Female	0	1	0	0

From this listing, you see that when Gender is equal to Male, the dummy variable Male is equal to 1; when Gender is equal to Female the dummy variable Male is equal to 0. Also, when Region is equal to West, all three dummy variables (North, East, and South) are equal to 0.

The next program uses PROC REG to run a regression using Total_Sales, and it uses the dummy variables for Gender and Region to predict Music_sales.

Program 9.8: Running PROG REG with Dummy Variables for Gender and Region

```
title "Running a Multiple Regression with Dummy Variables";
proc reg data=Dummy;
  model Music_Sales = Total_Sales Male North East South;
run;
quit;
```

The following output is the result:

Running a Multiple Regression with Dummy Variables

The REG Procedure
Model: MODEL1
Dependent Variable: Music_Sales

Number of Observations Read	200
Number of Observations Used	200

Analysis of Variance					
Source	DF	Sum of Squares	Mean Square	F Value	Pr > F
Model	5	19581	3916.26572	22.36	<.0001
Error	194	33978	175.14521		
Corrected Total	199	53559			

Root MSE	13.23424	R-Square	0.3656
Dependent Mean	75.45000	Adj R-Sq	0.3492
Coeff Var	17.54042		

Parameter Estimates					
Variable	DF	Parameter Estimate	Standard Error	t Value	Pr > |t|
Intercept	1	28.65896	7.90988	3.62	0.0004
Total_Sales	1	0.04028	0.00991	4.06	<.0001
Male	1	8.79970	1.94115	4.53	<.0001
North	1	15.58384	2.53144	6.16	<.0001
East	1	24.65112	2.91089	8.47	<.0001
South	1	14.03834	2.91496	4.82	<.0001

Looking at this output, you see that all of the predictor variables are significant. In practice, you would also need to look at your diagnostic plots and check for collinearity, which is the topic of the next section.

Detecting Collinearity

A major problem with multiple regression models is collinearity. If two or more predictor variables are highly correlated, and they are both entered into a regression model, you might get very unstable estimates of slopes. A popular method for assessing collinearity is the variance inflation factor (VIF). To compute the VIF for any of the predictor variables, you run a regression of all the other predictor variables to predict the one in question. For example, if you have predictor variables X1, X2, and X3, you run the following three regressions:

- X1 as a function of X2 and X3
- X2 as a function of X1 and X3
- X3 as a function of X1 and X2

Then you compute a multiple R-square for each of these models and compute the VIF:

$$VIF_i = 1/(1-R_i^2)$$

To have SAS compute the VIF for each of your predictor variables, you simply need to include VIF as an option on the MODEL statement. As an example, let's compute the VIF for each of the predictor variables in the `exercise` data set:

Program 9.9: Using the VIF to Detect Collinearity

```
title "Using the VIF to Detect Collinearity";
proc reg data=exercise;
  model Pushups = Age Rest_Pulse Max_Pulse Run_Pulse / VIF;
run;
quit;
```

Here is the portion of the output that shows the VIF:

			Parameter Estimates				
Variable	DF	Parameter Estimate	Standard Error	t Value	Pr > |t|	Variance Inflation
Intercept	1	93.56536	21.33252	4.39	<.0001	0
Age	1	-0.31264	0.10918	-2.86	0.0063	1.43496
Rest_Pulse	1	-0.02608	0.31565	-0.08	0.9345	4.34454
Max_Pulse	1	-1.26238	0.54665	-2.31	0.0256	11.59795
Run_Pulse	1	0.84388	0.45045	1.87	0.0675	8.19934

Values for VIF that are greater than 10 are considered large. You should also pay attention to VIF values between 5 and 10. In this example, you see large VIFs for Max_Pulse and Run_Pulse. At this point, you might consider leaving only one of these variables in the model or, perhaps, creating a new variable that is a linear combination of these two variables.

Influential Observations in Multiple Regression Models

In the previous chapter, you saw the various ways that PROC REG helps you identify influential observations. To see how you can identify such observations in a multiple regression model, the next example will predict the number of push-ups using the model Pushups=Max_Pulse Run_Pulse (one of the best models that satisfy Mallow's criteria), and then it will look for influential observations. Besides using the INFLUENCE option, ODS Graphics will be turned on.

Program 9.10: Detecting Influential Observations in Multiple Regression

```
ods graphics on;
title "Detecting Influential Observations in Multiple
Regression";
proc reg data=exercise
  plots(label only) = (cooksd
            rstudentbypredicted
            dffits
            dfbetas);
  id Subj;
  model Pushups = Age Max_Pulse Run_Pulse / influence;
run;
quit;
ods graphics off;
```

In this program, you include a PLOTS= option so that you can control exactly which plots get created and whether they are shown individually or in a panel. Because the options LABEL and ONLY are on the left-hand side of the equal sign, they apply to all the plots. LABEL says to use the value of the ID variable to label influential points on the plots. The ONLY option indicates that you do not want to produce any of the default plots. The following plots are selected:

Plot Name	Description
Cooksd	Cook's D statistic (the effect on the predicted value)
Rstudentbypredicted	Externally Studentized residuals by predicted value
DFFITS	The difference in the overall effect on the betas
DFBETAS	The difference on each beta (one computed for each variable)

Before you see the plots that this program produces, here is a screen capture of the Results window, after the option **Expand All** has been selected:

Remember, you need to double-click on a plot or panel to display it. You can also save these plots using the **Save As** option on the menu bar.

The following plots result from Program 9.10:

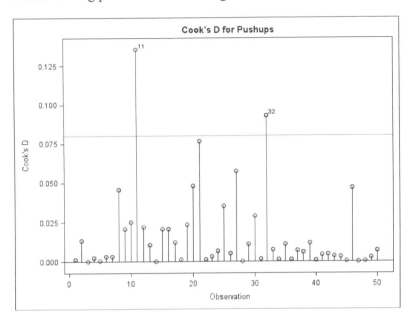

Notice that subjects 11 and 32 are labeled as being influential.

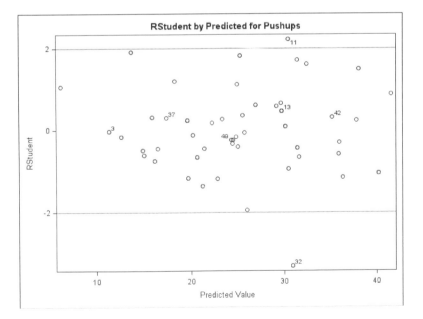

The same two subjects, 11 and 32, are also identified in this plot.

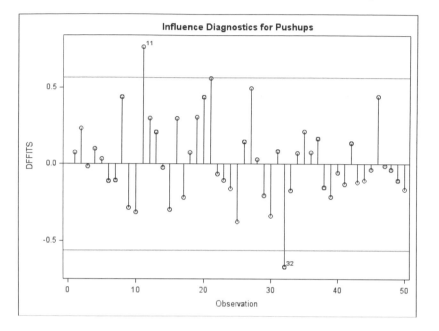

No surprise: here you see the same two subjects identified as influential.

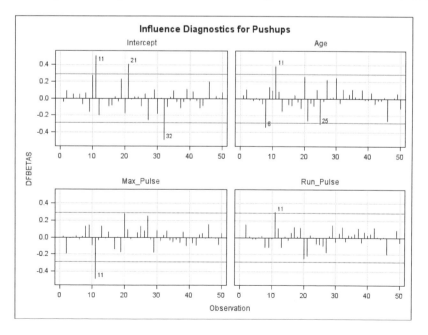

Because you did not include the UNPACK option for this plot, all four plots are shown on a single panel. Here you can see exactly which variables are contributing to a subject's influence. For example, it seems that the value of Age for subject 8 and the values for Age, Max_Pulse, and Run_Pulse for subject 11 are the reasons why these two subjects are identified as influential.

After you have identified influential observations, you need to decide on your next step. If possible, you should first try to determine whether any of the influential points are the result of data errors. If they are, you need to correct the errors and repeat the analysis. If the influential data points are not the result of data errors, you might want to investigate additional models that can account for these values (including, perhaps, some nonlinear terms).

If possible, you might also want to collect more data in the same area as the influential observations to determine whether the results are similar for other subjects. If you decide to run your analysis with certain influential observations removed, you need to state clearly in your discussion that these data values were removed and give a rationale for removing them. It is common to run an analysis with and without certain questionable data points to determine whether the major conclusions of the study are altered by these observations.

Conclusions

In this chapter, you learned how to run multiple regression models. You also saw several selection methods that work with small or very large data sets. You learned how ODS Graphics can help you to determine influential data points and to test the assumptions required for multiple regression. Finally, you saw the effect of collinearity on your multiple regression models and how to identify influential observations.

The next chapter deals with statistical techniques that are appropriate to categorical data.

Categorical Data

Categorical Data

Introduction

This chapter deals with categorical data analysis. You will learn how to compare proportions using the chi-square test and Fisher's exact test. You can use these tests with data in which each observation represents a single subject or with data that consists of frequency counts. To this end, a program and a useful SAS macro (don't be scared here) are presented.

Relative risk and odds ratios are commonly used to describe the results of cohort and case-control studies. You will see how SAS computes these quantities.

Finally, you will learn how to test one-way frequencies against a theoretical distribution.

Comparing Proportions

Data set `risk` contains information on risk factors for heart attacks (this is made up data for instructional purposes). This data set contains the following variables:

Variable Name	Description
Age_Group	Age category: 1=<60, 2=60-70, 3=71+
Gender	Gender: M=Male, F=Female
Age	Age in years
Chol	Cholesterol level
Heart_Attack	Heart attack: 1=Yes, 0=No (formatted as Yes and No)

To compare heart attack prevalence by gender, you would use the following program:

Program 10.1: Comparing Proportions Using Chi-Square

```
title "Comparing Proportions";
proc freq data=risk;
   tables Gender * Heart_Attack / chisq;
run;
```

To generate a table of Gender by Heart_Attack, you place an asterisk between those variables on your TABLES statement. In this program, Gender forms the rows of the table and Heart_Attack forms the columns.

To request a two-way table, use the following general form:

```
tables row-variable * column-variable / options;
```

The CHISQ option on the TABLES statement requests SAS to compute the chi-square statistic, along with several others. Here is the output:

Comparing Proportions

The FREQ Procedure

Frequency Percent Row Pct Col Pct	Table of Gender by Heart_Attack ❶		
		Heart_Attack	
Gender	No	Yes	Total
F	233 46.60 93.20 52.71	17 3.40 6.80 29.31	250 50.00
M	209 41.80 83.60 47.29	41 8.20 16.40 70.69	250 50.00
Total	442 88.40	58 11.60	500 100.00

Statistics for Table of Gender by Heart_Attack

Statistic	DF	Value	Prob	
Chi-Square	1	11.2342	0.0008	❷
Likelihood Ratio Chi-Square	1	11.5397	0.0007	
Continuity Adj. Chi-Square	1	10.3175	0.0013	
Mantel-Haenszel Chi-Square	1	11.2117	0.0008	
Phi Coefficient		0.1499		
Contingency Coefficient		0.1482		
Cramer's V		0.1499		

Fisher's Exact Test	
Cell (1,1) Frequency (F)	233
Left-sided Pr <= F	0.9998
Right-sided Pr >= F	5.815E-04
Table Probability (P)	3.804E-04
Two-sided Pr <= P	0.0012

Sample Size = 500

❶ The output starts with a 2x2 table with Gender as the rows and Heart_Attack as the columns. The box at the upper-left corner of the table is the key to the numbers in each cell of the table. The top number in each cell is the frequency. For example, there were 233 females who did not have a heart attack. The next number in the cell is a percentage. Of the 500 people in this study, 46.60% of them were females who did not have a heart attack. The third number in the cell is a row percentage. Of all the females, 93.20% did not have a heart attack. Finally, the last number in each cell is a column percentage. Of the 442 people who did not have a heart attack, 52.71% of them were female.

In this example, you are probably most interested in the row percent. You can see that 6.8% of the females had heart attacks, compared to 16.4% of the males.

❷ To determine whether this difference in proportions is statistically significant, you look at the value of chi-square (11.2342). With 1 degree of freedom (DF), the probability of obtaining a chi-square this large or larger, by chance, and assuming the null hypothesis of no difference, is p=.0008. Therefore, if your chosen level of alpha is .05, you reject the null hypotheses and conclude that the heart attack prevalence rates for males and females are not equal.

The following table describes commonly used options on the TABLES statement:

Option	Description
AGREE	Kappa coefficient of agreement
ALL	A quick way to get CHISQ, MEASURES, and CMH
CHISQ	Computes chi-square, Fisher's exact (for 2x2), and several other tests
CMH	Cochran-Mantel-Haenszel statistics
FISHER	Fisher's exact test (needed only for tables larger than 2x2)
MEASURES	Various measures of association, such as Pearson and Spearman coefficients
RELRISK	Computes relative risk (also called risk ratio)
TREND	Computes Cochran-Armitage test for trend

Rearranging Rows and Columns in a Table

One of the first things you might have noticed in the previous output is that the order of the columns seems backwards. You might prefer that the Yes column appear before the No column. If you want to compute a relative risk of men compared to women, you might also prefer that the top row be the frequencies for males. As you saw in Chapter 3, one way to rearrange the rows and columns in a table is to format both variables and to use the ORDER=FORMATTED option on the PROC FREQ statement. The following program uses this method to rearrange the rows and columns in the previous table:

Program 10.2: Rearranging Rows and Columns in a Table and Computing Relative Risk

```
proc format;
   value $gen 'M' = '1:Male'
              'F' = '2:Female';
   value attack 1 = '1:Yes'
                0 = '2:No';
run;

title "Reordering the Rows and Columns in a 2x2 Table";
proc freq data=risk order=formatted;
   tables Gender * Heart_Attack / chisq relrisk;
   format Gender $gen. Heart_Attack attack.;
run;
```

You start by creating two temporary formats, one for Gender and one for Heart_Attack. The trick used here is to arrange the format values so that they are in alphabetical order, which corresponds to the order in which you want your table rows and columns.

Remember that the default ordering of tables in PROC FREQ is by the internal value of the variables, and not by the formatted values. Therefore, you need to use the ORDER=FORMATTED option if you want the rows and columns to be arranged by the formatted values. Just making the formats is not enough—you need to associate the two formats with the corresponding variables in a FORMAT statement. Finally, in this program, the option RELRISK was added so that SAS would compute relative risk and odds ratios.

A cohort study typically compares some outcome, such as having a heart attack, between two or more groups. For example, you might compare heart attack rates between people with cholesterol levels above 140 to heart attack rates of people with cholesterol levels below 140. One way to report your results is to compare the incidence rates (the proportion of people who have a heart attack) between the two groups. The ratio of incidence rates is called the relative risk (also called a risk ratio).

A case-control study starts with a group of subjects that have a given outcome (cases) and a group of people who do not have the outcome (controls). For example, suppose you want to study possible causes for leukemia in children. This disease is relatively rare, so a cohort study would be impractical (you would need to compare very large groups of subjects in order to have enough subjects who develop the disease). Instead, you would use a cancer registry to identify a group of children with leukemia. Next, you would identify a similar group of children who do not have leukemia. Finally, you would compare risk factors, such as exposure to toxic chemicals, between the two groups. One way to report your results is to compare the odds of disease in the group that was exposed to toxic chemicals (the cases) to the odds of disease in the group that was not exposed to toxic chemicals (the controls). The ratio of these odds is called an odds ratio.

In a case-control study, you can use the odds ratio as an estimate of the relative risk. This estimate is more accurate when the incidence rates are low (which is usually the reason for doing a case-control study in the first place). When you get SAS to compute statistics for a 2x2 table, it computes both relative risk and odds ratios. Based on your study design, you decide which one to use.

Here are portions of the output:

Reordering the Rows and Columns in a 2x2 Table

The FREQ Procedure

Frequency Percent Row Pct Col Pct	Table of Gender by Heart_Attack		
		Heart_Attack	
Gender	1:Yes	2:No	Total
1:Male	41	209	250
	8.20	41.80	50.00
	16.40	83.60	
	70.69	47.29	
2:Female	17	233	250
	3.40	46.60	50.00
	6.80	93.20	
	29.31	52.71	
Total	58	442	500
	11.60	88.40	100.00

You can see that the rows and columns of the table are in the new order. Next is the portion of the output that shows the relative risk and odds ratio:

Estimates of the Relative Risk (Row1/Row2)			
Type of Study	Value	95% Confidence Limits	
Case-Control (Odds Ratio)	2.6887	1.4824	4.8768
Cohort (Col1 Risk)	2.4118	1.4089	4.1284
Cohort (Col2 Risk)	0.8970	0.8411	0.9566

If this were a cohort study, the relative risk for a man having a heart attack compared to that of a woman would be 2.4118 (95%CI 1.4098, 4.1284). Because the 95% CI does not include 1, you would report this as a statistically significant result at the .05 level. The last row of output is labeled Col2 Risk. This is the relative risk for men not having a heart attack (column 2).

If this were a case-control study instead of a cohort study, you would report the odds ratio as 2.6887 (with a 95% CI of 1.4824 to 4.8768).

Tables with Expected Values Less Than 5 (Fisher's Exact Test)

If you have tables in which more than 20% of the cells have expected values that are less than 5, computing chi-square might not be appropriate. For 2x2 tables, two options are to use Yates' correction for continuity or Fisher's exact test. SAS does both automatically. For larger tables, you can request Fisher's exact test if the table is not too large (computation time can become excessive for larger tables), or you can collapse cells in the table so that the cell frequencies are larger.

To demonstrate how SAS deals with small expected frequencies for 2x2 tables, the next program creates a small data set and then runs PROC FREQ:

Program 10.3: Tables with Small Expected Frequencies–Fisher's Exact Test

```
data small_counts;
   input Group $ Outcome $ @@;
datalines;
A Good A Good A Good A Poor A Good A Good
B Poor B Poor B Good B Poor B Poor
;
title "Tables with Small Expected Frequencies";
proc freq data=small_counts;
   tables Group * Outcome / chisq;
run;
```

The short DATA step creates a SAS data set called small_counts. The two at signs (@@) on the INPUT statement let you create several observations from a single line of data.

Each time SAS reaches the bottom of the DATA step, it moves to the next line of data (if you omitted the two at signs in this program, data set small_counts would have only 2 observations). The double trailing at signs is an instruction to SAS to "hold the line" and not go to the next line of data when you reach the bottom of the DATA step.

Here is the output from Program 10.3:

Tables with Small Expected Frequencies

The FREQ Procedure

Frequency Percent Row Pct Col Pct	Table of Group by Outcome		
		Outcome	
Group	Good	Poor	Total
A	5	1	6
	45.45	9.09	54.55
	83.33	16.67	
	83.33	20.00	
B	1	4	5
	9.09	36.36	45.45
	20.00	80.00	
	16.67	80.00	
Total	6	5	11
	54.55	45.45	100.00

Statistics for Table of Group by Outcome

Statistic	DF	Value	Prob
Chi-Square	1	4.4122	0.0357
Likelihood Ratio Chi-Square	1	4.7474	0.0293
Continuity Adj. Chi-Square	1	2.2275	0.1356
Mantel-Haenszel Chi-Square	1	4.0111	0.0452
Phi Coefficient		0.6333	
Contingency Coefficient		0.5351	
Cramer's V		0.6333	

WARNING: 100% of the cells have expected counts less than 5. Chi-Square may not be a valid test.

Fisher's Exact Test	
Cell (1,1) Frequency (F)	5
Left-sided Pr <= F	0.9978
Right-sided Pr >= F	0.0671
Table Probability (P)	0.0649
Two-sided Pr <= P	0.0801

Sample Size = 11

Notice that SAS prints a warning when more than 20% of the cells have expected values that are less than 5. In this case, the chi-square value and resulting probability are not valid. The row in the output labeled Continuity Adj. Chi-Square is the Yates' corrected value (2.2275). Under the heading Fisher's Exact Test, you see the two-sided probability equal to .0801. If you were conducting a hypothesis test with alpha set to the usual value of .05, you would fail to reject the null hypothesis that the proportion of good outcomes was equal in the two groups. In practice, you might report that group A seemed to have a higher percentage of good outcomes, although the percentage did not reach statistical significance. At this point, you would suggest that more research was needed (perhaps with a larger sample), and that you would like some more grant money so that you can continue investigating this problem.

Computing Chi-Square from Frequency Data

Maybe you already have a 2x2 table, and you want SAS to compute chi-square (or some other statistic). For example, suppose you are given the following table:

	Sick	Well
Placebo	30	10
Drug	15	40

To get SAS to compute statistics for this table, you need to use a WEIGHT statement and specify the frequencies for each combination of drug group and outcome. Program 10.4 shows how to use the WEIGHT statement:

Program 10.4: Computing Chi-Square from Frequency Data

```
data frequencies;
   input Treatment $ Outcome $ Count;
datalines;
Placebo Sick 30
Placebo Well 10
Drug Sick 15
Drug Well 40
;
title "Computing Chi_Square from Frequency Data";
proc freq data=frequencies;
   tables Treatment * Outcome / chisq;
   weight Count;
run;
```

The short DATA step creates a SAS data set with four observations and three variables. Here is the data set:

Listing of Data Set FREQUENCIES

Treatment	Outcome	Count
Placebo	Sick	30
Placebo	Well	10
Drug	Sick	15
Drug	Well	40

You include a WEIGHT statement in PROC FREQ. The WEIGHT statement tells the procedure to use the values of the variable Count as the frequencies that correspond to each combination of Treatment and Outcome. Here is a portion of the output:

Computing Chi_Square from Frequency Data

The FREQ Procedure

Frequency Percent Row Pct Col Pct	Table of Treatment by Outcome		
		Outcome	
Treatment	Sick	Well	Total
Drug	15	40	55
	15.79	42.11	57.89
	27.27	72.73	
	33.33	80.00	
Placebo	30	10	40
	31.58	10.53	42.11
	75.00	25.00	
	66.67	20.00	
Total	45	50	95
	47.37	52.63	100.00

Using a Chi-Square Macro

SAS macros are pre-packaged pieces of SAS code or entire programs that enable you to perform routine tasks more easily. Although *writing* macros is considered an advanced topic, *using* them is really quite simple. So, with that in mind, you can copy the code for this macro from the SAS Web site and use it any time you need to compute chi-square for a 2x2 table, when you already have cell frequencies.

Program 10.5 contains the macro code:

Program 10.5: A SAS Macro for Computing Chi-Square from Cell Frequencies

```
/************************************************************
Macro CHISQ
Purpose: To compute chi-square (and any other valid
         PROC FREQ TABLES options) from frequencies in a
         2 x 2 table.
Sample Calling Sequencies;
    %CHISQ(10,20,30,40)
    %CHISQ(10,20,30,40,OPTIONS=CMH)
    %CHISQ(10,20,30,40,OPTIONS=CHISQ CMH)
************************************************************/
%macro chisq(a,b,c,d,options=chisq);
    data chisq;
        array cells[2,2] _temporary_ (&a &b &c &d);
        do row = 1 to 2;
            do Col = 1 to 2;
                Count = cells[Row,Col];
                output;
            end;
        end;
    run;
    proc freq data=chisq;
        tables Row*Col / &options;
        weight Count;
    run;
%mend chisq;
```

To demonstrate how to use this macro, suppose you copy this program to a folder called C:\SASPROGS\MACROS and name the file CHISQ.SAS. You then have several choices. One is to open the file in the editor window of SAS Display Manager and submit it. The other is to issue the following command:

```
%include 'c:\sasprogs\macros\chisq.sas';
```

After you issue the command, click the Submit icon. Now the macro is ready to be used. If the four cell frequencies of your table are 30,10, 15, and 40 (in the order top left, top right, bottom left, bottom right), you would submit the following line:

```
%chisq(30,10,15,40)
```

SAS will produce the same output that you saw in Program 10.4. Notice that this macro call (calling a macro is the SAS terminology for running a macro) does not end in a semicolon. In this example, a semicolon at the end of the macro call would not actually do any harm. However, it is considered by some to be poor programming.

If you want to compute other statistics such as relative risks or Mantel-Haenszel chi-square, you can request these options by including an OPTIONS= argument when you call the macro, like this:

```
%chisq(30,10,15,40,options=risk cmh)
```

A Short-Cut Method for Requesting Multiple Tables

There is a convenient way to request multiple tables using the TABLES statement. The statement:

```
tables A * B;
```

creates a single table of variable A (rows) by variable B (columns). The statement:

```
tables A * (B C D);
```

creates three tables—A by B, A by C, and A by D.

The statement:

```
tables (A B) * (C D);
```

creates four tables—A by C, A by D, B by C and B by D (in other words, every variable in the first list by every variable in the second list).

You can also request three-way tables (page by row by column) with the statement:

```
tables A * B * C;
```

This statement creates tables of B by C for each separate value of A. Each one of the tables will be on a separate page.

Computing Coefficient Kappa—A Test of Agreement

The AGREE option on the TABLES statement computes the Kappa coefficient, also known as a coefficient of agreement. For example, suppose two psychiatrists are evaluating the same patients, and each one decides whether each patient has attention deficit disorder. By chance alone, the two raters might agree or disagree on any individual diagnosis. For example, if the probability of a positive diagnosis is 50%, they will agree 50% of the time, by chance alone. Coefficient Kappa adjusts for the chance agreement.

The following program shows how you can compute Kappa on data from two raters:

Program 10.6: Computing Kappa Coefficient of Agreement

```
data kappa;
      input Rater1 : $1. Rater2 : $1. @@;
datalines;
Y Y N N Y N N Y Y Y Y Y Y Y Y N N N N N N Y Y Y N Y Y Y N N N Y N
N N N N
Y Y Y Y N N N N Y N Y Y Y Y Y N N N N N N N N Y Y N N Y Y Y N N
;
title "Computing Coefficient Kappa";
proc freq data=kappa;
      tables Rater1 * Rater2 / agree;
      test kappa;
run;
```

The short DATA step creates a data set with two variables (Rater1 and Rater2) and 33 observations (see the discussion about Program 10.3 for an explanation of the double at sign on the INPUT statement). The colon in the INPUT statement also needs some explanation. When you use list input (appropriate for data values that are separated by delimiters), you can simply provide a list of variables on the INPUT statement. If you want to create a character variable, you follow the variable name with a dollar sign ($). When you do this, SAS needs to determine the storage length of that character variable. The default length of a character variable when you are using list input is 8 bytes.

You can override this default value in two convenient ways: one is to follow the variable name with a colon, followed by an informat. That method is used in Program 10.6. The other method is to include an INFORMAT statement before the INPUT statement, which associates each of your variables with the informat that you want to use (very similar to a FORMAT statement, in which you associate variables with formats).

The AGREE option computes Kappa. The TEST statement provides a hypothesis test for Kappa, testing whether it is significantly different from 0 (and is therefore better than chance). Here is the output:

Computing Coefficient Kappa

The FREQ Procedure

Frequency Percent Row Pct Col Pct	Table of Rater1 by Rater2			
		Rater2		
	Rater1	N	Y	Total
	N	16	2	18
		48.48	6.06	54.55
		88.89	11.11	
		84.21	14.29	
	Y	3	12	15
		9.09	36.36	45.45
		20.00	80.00	
		15.79	85.71	
	Total	19	14	33
		57.58	42.42	100.00

Statistics for Table of Rater1 by Rater2

McNemar's Test	
Statistic (S)	0.2000
DF	1
Pr > S	0.6547

Simple Kappa Coefficient	
Kappa	0.6927
ASE	0.1262
95% Lower Conf Limit	0.4453
95% Upper Conf Limit	0.9402

Test of H0: Kappa = 0	
ASE under H0	0.1737
Z	3.9870
One-sided Pr > Z	<.0001
Two-sided Pr > |Z|	<.0001

Sample Size = 33

A Kappa value of 1 indicates perfect agreement, and a Kappa value of 0 indicates that the agreement is attributable to chance. It is possible for Kappa to be negative; agreement can be less than chance. You see from this output that Kappa is equal to .6927. A two-tailed hypothesis test for Kappa equal to zero yields a p-value <.0001. You can conclude that the agreement between the two raters was significant and not due to chance.

Computing Tests for Trends

If one or both of your variables is ordinal (as opposed to nominal), you might want to compute a chi-square test for trend. You have a choice here: you can choose to use a Cochran-Mantel-Haenszel chi-square or the Cochran-Armitage test for trend.

The next example demonstrates both tests. Assume that you have frequencies of success and failure for four doses of a drug. Because the doses are in increasing order, you can add more "horsepower" by using tests for trend rather than just using a simple chi-square statistic. The following table summarizes the results of a hypothetical study:

		Dose			
		1	2	3	4
Outcome	Success	8	8	10	15
	Failure	12	12	10	5
		20	20	20	20

Notice that the success rate appears to increase with increasing doses. You can run the following program to test this trend:

Program 10.7: Demonstrating Two Tests for Trend

```
data trend;
   input Outcome $ Dose Count;
datalines;
Success 1 8
Success 2 8
Success 3 10
Success 4 15
Failure 1 12
Failure 2 12
Failure 3 10
Failure 4 5
;
title "Computing Tests for Trend";
proc freq data=trend;
   tables Outcome * Dose / cmh trend;
   weight Count;
run;
```

Here is a portion of the output:

Computing Tests for Trend

The FREQ Procedure

Frequency Percent Row Pct Col Pct	Table of Outcome by Dose				
		Dose			
Outcome	1	2	3	4	Total
Failure	12	12	10	5	39
	15.00	15.00	12.50	6.25	48.75
	30.77	30.77	25.64	12.82	
	60.00	60.00	50.00	25.00	
Success	8	8	10	15	41
	10.00	10.00	12.50	18.75	51.25
	19.51	19.51	24.39	36.59	
	40.00	40.00	50.00	75.00	
Total	20	20	20	20	80
	25.00	25.00	25.00	25.00	100.00

Statistics for Table of Outcome by Dose

Cochran-Armitage Trend Test	
Statistic (Z)	-2.3007
One-sided Pr < Z	0.0107
Two-sided Pr > |Z|	0.0214

Sample Size = 80

Summary Statistics for Outcome by Dose

Cochran-Mantel-Haenszel Statistics (Based on Table Scores)				
Statistic	Alternative Hypothesis	DF	Value	Prob
1	Nonzero Correlation	1	5.2271	0.0222
2	Row Mean Scores Differ	1	5.2271	0.0222
3	General Association	3	6.4722	0.0908

Total Sample Size = 80

The Cochran-Armitage test yields a p-value of .0214 and the Cochran-Mantel-Haenszel test yields a p-value of .0222. Both of these tests indicate that the success rate increases with increasing doses. A chi-square test on this same table yields a p-value of .0876 (typically interpreted as not significant). For more details about the other statistics produced by this option, refer to the SAS OnlineDoc.

Computing Chi-Square for One-Way Tables

You can use two options on the TABLES statement, TESTP= (test proportions) and TESTF= (test frequencies), to specify expected proportions or frequencies for each level in a one-way table.

For example, in the United States, the distribution of blood types is approximately:

O=45%, A=40%, B=11%, and AB=4%

Suppose you sample 200 people and obtain the following frequencies for blood types:

O=88, A=76, B=24, AB=12

What is the probability that this sample comes from a distribution of blood groups found in the United States?

On the TESTP= option, you can enter expected proportions either as numbers less than 1 (which must add to 1), or as percentages (which must add to 100%). The TESTF= option enables you to enter expected frequencies. You enter the proportions or frequencies in parentheses, and you separate them by spaces or commas. The following program analyzes the blood count data:

Program 10.8: Computing Chi-Square for a One-Way Table

```
data bloodtype;
   input Type $ Count @@;
datalines;
O 88 A 76 B 24 AB 12
;
title "Computing Chi-Square for a One-Way Table";
proc freq data=bloodtype;
   tables Type / testp = (.40 .04 .11 .45);
   weight Count;
run;
```

Because the blood counts are expressed as frequencies, you need to use the WEIGHT statement in PROC FREQ to tell the program to use the frequencies in the variable Count. Also (and this is very important), the order of the four theoretical proportions on the TESTP= option are in the alphabetical order of the four blood types. The TESTP= option could also have been written with percentages, like this:

```
tables Type / testp = (40 04 11 45);
```

Here is the output:

Computing Chi-Square for a One-Way Table

The FREQ Procedure

type	Frequency	Percent	Test Percent	Cumulative Frequency	Cumulative Percent
A	76	38.00	40.00	76	38.00
AB	12	6.00	4.00	88	44.00
B	24	12.00	11.00	112	56.00
O	88	44.00	45.00	200	100.00

Chi-Square Test for Specified Proportions	
Chi-Square	2.4263
DF	3
Pr > ChiSq	0.4888

Sample Size = 200

Looking at this output, you do not reject the null hypothesis that these 200 people have the same distribution of blood types as those found in the United States.

Conclusions

In this chapter, you learned how to compare proportions using PROC FREQ and how to compute relative risk and odds ratios. Because the order of the rows and columns in your table are important for many of the tests of association, you can use formats to control the order of the output. When one or both of your variables are ordinal, SAS provides several tests for trend. You learned how to use the AGREE option on your PROC FREQ TABLES statement to compute Kappa, a measure of inter-rater agreement. Finally, you learned that PROC FREQ can test frequencies in a one-way table against a theoretical distribution.

When you have several categorical predictor variables or a combination of categorical and continuous numeric predictor variables, you can use logistic regression to help you predict the probability of a particular outcome. In addition, you can see how each predictor variable influences the outcome by examining the odds ratios. The next chapter covers these topics.

Binary Logistic Regression

Introduction

This chapter demonstrates how to run logistic regression models using SAS. The chapter starts with a simple example with categorical predictors. Then continuous variables are added. The final example is a logistic regression model that includes interactions. Examples in this chapter cover only logistic regression with binary outcome variables.

You can find examples of multinomial or ordinal outcomes in the SAS OnlineDoc or in several publications from SAS Publishing, including *Logistic Regression Using SAS: Theory and Application* by Paul Allison and the *SAS/STAT User's Guide*, both of which are particularly recommended.

Some of the logistic regression models in this chapter use the data set `risk`, which was used in the previous chapter. This data set contains information about risk factors for heart attacks (the data is made-up for instructional purposes). The following variables are in this data set:

Variable Name	Description
Age_Group	Age category: 1=<60, 2=60-70, 3=71+
Gender	Gender: M=Male, F=Female
Age	Age in years
Chol	Cholesterol level
Heart_Attack	Heart attack: 1=Yes, 0=No (formatted as Yes and No)

Running a Logistic Regression Model with One Categorical Predictor Variable

This first example shows how to run a logistic regression model predicting heart attack as the outcome with Gender as a single predictor variable.

Program 11.1: Logistic Regression with One Categorical Predictor Variable

```
title "Logistic Regression with One Categorical Predictor Variable";
proc logistic data=risk;
   class Gender (param=ref ref='F');
   model Heart_Attack (event='Yes')= Gender / clodds = pl;
run;
quit;
```

This MODEL statement is similar to the MODEL statement of PROC REG. On the left-hand side of the equal sign, you specify your outcome variable, and on the right-hand side, you list one or more predictor variables.

The EVENT='Yes' option on the MODEL statement says that you want to predict the probability of having a heart attack. Because the variable Heart_Attack is formatted as Yes and No, you use EVENT='Yes' if you want to predict the probability of having a heart attack. If you wanted to predict the probability of not having a heart attack, you would use EVENT='No'.

If you do not supply a value for the EVENT option, the procedure will, by default, use the first value of the outcome as determined by the alphabetical or numerical ordering of the outcome variable. In this example, omitting the EVENT option would result in the model predicting the probability of not having a heart attack (because No comes before Yes alphabetically). It is a good idea to always use the EVENT= option.

If you have a numeric outcome variable that is not formatted, you still need to place quotes around the event value. For example, if you have a variable called Outcome with values of 0 and 1 and you want to predict the probability of a 1, you would use:

```
model Outcome (event = '1') = predictor variable(s);
```

The CLODDS=PL option indicates that you want SAS to compute confidence limits on the odds ratio using the method of profile likelihood. The profile likelihood ratios require much more computation than the default Wald-based intervals but are preferred to the Wald intervals, especially for sample sizes that are less than 50 (Allison 1999).

Next, because Gender is a categorical variable, it is listed on a CLASS statement. An extremely useful feature of PROC LOGISTIC is that it creates dummy variables (also called design variables) for you automatically. You can create these dummy variables in several ways. Two of the more popular methods are called effect coding and reference coding. Effect coding uses the mean level of the predictor variable as the reference level, and reference coding uses a single value of the predictor variable as a reference.

The option PARAM=REF (parameterization) says that you want to use reference coding for your dummy variable. You also have the option of choosing the reference level, which is accomplished in this example by setting REF='F' (causing females to be the reference level). If your CLASS variable is formatted, use the formatted value when you enter the reference level. The order of the categories of CLASS variables is determined by the formatted values of these variables (if you have supplied a format). Also, if you do not supply a reference level, the last value is used. In this example in which the values of Gender are M and F, the last value is M because M comes after F in the collating sequence.

The output from this procedure is displayed in sections:

Logistic Regression with One Categorical Predictor Variable

The LOGISTIC Procedure

Model Information	
Data Set	WORK.RISK
Response Variable	Heart_Attack
Number of Response Levels	2
Model	binary logit
Optimization Technique	Fisher's scoring

Number of Observations Read	500	❶
Number of Observations Used	500	

Response Profile ❷		
Ordered Value	Heart_Attack	Total Frequency
1	No	442
2	Yes	58

Probability modeled is Heart_Attack='Yes'.

Class Level Information ❸		
Class	Value	Design Variables
Gender	F	0
	M	1

Model Convergence Status
Convergence criterion (GCONV=1E-8) satisfied.

You need to pay particular attention to this section of the output, because it is important to be sure that you are modeling the correct value for your outcome and that your dummy variables are created with the reference levels that you want. ❶ First, you see the number of observations that were read and used. These numbers will differ if you have any missing values for the outcome variable or for any of the predictors. ❷ Next, you see that

the ordered values are `Yes` and `No` and that the probability being modeled is
Heart_Attack='Yes'. ❸ Finally, you see how PROC LOGISTIC created the reference-
coded dummy variable for Gender. Because you chose `F` as the reference level, that value
was given a zero.

Model Fit Statistics		
Criterion	Intercept Only	Intercept and Covariates
AIC	360.879	351.339
SC	365.093	359.768
-2 Log L	358.879	347.339

This next section provides you with three indicators of fit statistics. Both the AIC
(Akaike Information Criterion) and SC (Schwartz Criteria) adjust for the number of
predictors in the model (the smaller this value is, the better). These values provide you
with a way to compare competing models. Another indicator of fit is -2 Log L, with
smaller values indicating a better fit. This value, however, is not adjusted for the number
of predictor variables in your model.

Testing Global Null Hypothesis: BETA=0 ❶			
Test	Chi-Square	DF	Pr > ChiSq
Likelihood Ratio	11.5397	1	0.0007
Score	11.2342	1	0.0008
Wald	10.5994	1	0.0011

Type 3 Analysis of Effects ❷			
Effect	DF	Wald Chi-Square	Pr > ChiSq
Gender	1	10.5994	0.0011

Analysis of Maximum Likelihood Estimates ❸						
Parameter		DF	Estimate	Standard Error	Wald Chi-Square	Pr > ChiSq
Intercept		1	-2.6178	0.2512	108.5792	<.0001
Gender	M	1	0.9890	0.3038	10.5994	0.0011

❶ This section gives you several different methods for testing the null hypothesis that beta=0. Using any of these methods, you reject the null hypothesis at the .05 level of significance. ❷ Because this model has only one predictor variable, the p-value for Gender is equal to the Wald value testing the global hypothesis. ❸ Here you see the intercept and the parameter estimates for the Gender dummy variable. The log odds of having a heart attack is equal to -2.6178 + .9890 x Gender (where Gender is 0 for females and 1 for males). Note that the test for Gender here is again a Wald test, equal to the preceding ones.

Odds Ratio Estimates ❶			
Effect	Point Estimate	95% Wald Confidence Limits	
Gender M vs F	2.689	1.482	4.877

Association of Predicted Probabilities and Observed Responses ❷			
Percent Concordant	37.3	Somers' D	0.234
Percent Discordant	13.9	Gamma	0.458
Percent Tied	48.9	Tau-a	0.048
Pairs	25636	c	0.617

Profile Likelihood Confidence Interval for Odds Ratios ❸				
Effect	Unit	Estimate	95% Confidence Limits	
Gender M vs F	1.0000	2.689	1.507	4.994

❶ This section starts with an estimate of the odds ratio for Gender, along with the 95% CI. These are the Wald estimates, based on a normal approximation. (The profile likelihood estimates are displayed in a later section of the output.) Because females are the reference level, this odds ratio means that the odds of a male having a heart attack are 2.689 times that for a female.

❷ Next, there are several measures that help you determine how well the model is doing. The first four values in the column on the left are computed as follows: start by taking all possible pairs of subjects in which one has the outcome in question and the other does not. Because there were 58 subjects who had heart attacks and 442 who did not, the number of possible pairs is 58 x 442=25,636. For each of these pairs, compute the probability of each person in the pair having a heart attack, based on the model. If the prediction is in the same direction as the actual pair (i.e. the person with the higher probability is the one who had the heart attack), then that pair is labeled concordant. If not, the pair is labeled discordant. If the probabilities are computed to be the same (because this example has just Gender in the model, the probabilities will be the same if both subjects in the pair are the same sex), the pair is called tied. In this simple example, the predicted probability of a heart attack for men is higher than that for women, so pairs in which the man had a heart attack and the women didn't are concordant, but pairs in which the women had a heart attack and the man did not are discordant.

The four values in the column on the right are all measures of rank correlation and are computed from the concordant, discordant, and tied pairs. Models with higher values of these measures of association have better predictive value than models with lower values of these measures. The c statistic estimates the probability that an observation with the outcome will have a higher probability than will an observation without the outcome. In this example, the probability is .617 that a person who had a heart attack has a higher predicted probability than does a person who did not have a heart attack. The c statistic also gives you the area under a Receiver Operating Characteristic (ROC) curve (discussed at the end of this chapter).

❸ Because of the CLODDS=PL option on the MODEL statement, you see the profile likelihood estimates here. In this example, the point estimate is the same as the Wald estimate shown previously in the output, but the confidence interval is slightly different.

Running a Logistic Regression Model with One Continuous Predictor Variable

You can include continuous predictor variables in your logistic regression models. The MODEL statement looks similar to the ones you used for multiple regression.

In this example, you will use cholesterol level (variable Chol) as a predictor of heart attack. Here is the program:

Program 11.2: Logistic Regression with One Continuous Predictor Variable

```
title "Logistic Regression with One Continuous Predictor Variable";
proc logistic data=risk;
   model Heart_Attack (event='Yes') = Chol / clodds = pl;
   units Chol = 10;
run;
quit;
```

Because this model does not have categorical variables, this program does not include a CLASS statement. A UNITS statement was included. Without a UNITS statement, the odds ratios shown in the output would represent the increase in the odds of having a heart attack for each unit increase in cholesterol. In this program, you are asking for the odds ratio for each increase of 10 units. You can include as many variables and units as you want on one UNITS statement.

Here are some selected portions of the output:

Model Fit Statistics		
Criterion	Intercept Only	Intercept and Covariates
AIC	360.879	345.989
SC	365.093	354.418
-2 Log L	358.879	341.989

Testing Global Null Hypothesis: BETA=0			
Test	Chi-Square	DF	Pr > ChiSq
Likelihood Ratio	16.8901	1	<.0001
Score	16.1835	1	<.0001
Wald	15.4836	1	<.0001

Analysis of Maximum Likelihood Estimates					
Parameter	DF	Estimate	Standard Error	Wald Chi-Square	Pr > ChiSq
Intercept	1	-5.9979	1.0494	32.6651	<.0001
Chol	1	0.0192	0.00488	15.4836	<.0001

By examining this output, you see that cholesterol level is significant.

Odds Ratio Estimates			
Effect	Point Estimate	95% Wald Confidence Limits	
Chol	1.019	1.010	1.029 ❶

Association of Predicted Probabilities and Observed Responses ❷			
Percent Concordant	66.0	Somers' D	0.329
Percent Discordant	33.0	Gamma	0.333
Percent Tied	1.0	Tau-a	0.068
Pairs	25636	c	0.665

Profile Likelihood Confidence Interval for Odds Ratios ❸			
Effect	Unit	Estimate	95% Confidence Limits
Chol	10.0000	1.212	1.104	1.337

❶ You see the odds ratio for an increase of one unit of cholesterol, along with the 95% CI. (The odds ratio for 10 units of cholesterol is shown later in the output.) ❷ The percent of concordant pairs is much higher than the model that uses Gender as the predictor variable, and only 1% of the pairs were tied. The reason for the small percentage of tied pairs is that it is unlikely for the two people in each pair to have exactly the same cholesterol level. ❸ Here you see the effect of the UNITS statement. The odds ratio for an increase of 10 units of cholesterol is 1.212 with the 95% CI (1.104, 1.337).

Using a Format to Create a Categorical Variable from a Continuous Variable

There are times when you would prefer to place a continuous variable into groups. This arrangement would be especially important if you were expecting a nonlinear response for this variable.

You can use a DATA step to create this new categorical variable, or you can save some time and effort and use a format. CLASS variables in PROC LOGISTIC use formatted values, so all you have to do is provide a format for a continuous variable. In this example, you want to create two categories for cholesterol: Low to Medium and High. Program 11.3 demonstrates this:

Program 11.3: Using a Format to Create a Categorical Variable

```
proc format;
   value cholgrp low-200   = 'Low to Medium'
                 201-high = 'High';
run;

title "Using a Format to Create a Categorical Variable";
proc logistic data=risk;
   class Chol (param=ref ref='Low to Medium');
   model Heart_Attack (event='Yes') = Chol / clodds = pl;
   format Chol cholgrp.;
run;
quit;
```

First you need to create a format for the cholesterol groups. Next, because you are treating cholesterol groups as categories, you need a CLASS statement. In this example, the Low to Medium group is chosen as the reference level. Finally, and this is important, include a FORMAT statement in the procedure, associating the CHOLGRP format with the variable Chol.

Now let's look at some portions of the output:

Class Level Information ❶		
Class	Value	Design Variables
Chol	High	1
	Low to Medium	0

Model Convergence Status
Convergence criterion (GCONV=1E-8) satisfied.

Model Fit Statistics ❷		
Criterion	Intercept Only	Intercept and Covariates
AIC	360.879	345.878
SC	365.093	354.307
-2 Log L	358.879	341.878

Analysis of Maximum Likelihood Estimates						
Parameter		DF	Estimate	Standard Error	Wald Chi-Square	Pr > ChiSq
Intercept		1	-2.8032	0.2752	103.7386	<.0001
Chol	High	1	1.2356	0.3213	14.7908	0.0001 ❸

Odds Ratio Estimates ❹		
Effect	Point Estimate	95% Wald Confidence Limits
Chol High vs Low to Medium	3.440	1.833 6.458

Association of Predicted Probabilities and Observed Responses ❺			
Percent Concordant	39.6	Somers' D	0.281
Percent Discordant	11.5	Gamma	0.550
Percent Tied	48.8	Tau-a	0.058
Pairs	25636	c	0.641

Profile Likelihood Confidence Interval for Odds Ratios			
Effect	Unit	Estimate	95% Confidence Limits
Chol High vs Low to Medium	1.0000	3.440	1.878 6.678

❶ Cholesterol is now treated as a categorical variable with the reference level set at Low to Medium. ❷ The fit statistics are shown here. ❸ The parameter estimate (beta) is highly significant. ❹ The odds ratio is 3.44 for people in the High group compared to people in the Low to Medium group. ❺ Because there are now only two cholesterol groups, the probability of a tied pair is very high.

Using a Combination of Categorical and Continuous Variables in a Logistic Regression Model

The next program uses age group (Age_Group) and Gender as categorical variables and cholesterol (Chol) as a continuous variable to predict whether a person is going to have a heart attack.

Program 11.4: Using a Combination of Categorical and Continuous Variables

```
ods graphics on;
title "Using a Combination of Categorical and Continuous Variables";
proc logistic data=risk;
   class Age_Group (ref='1:< 60')
                 Gender (ref='F') / param=ref;
   model Heart_Attack (event='Yes') = Gender Age_Group Chol /
                                       clodds = pl;
   units Chol=10;
run;
quit;
ods graphics off;
```

You name the two categorical variables on the CLASS statement and indicate the reference levels for each. When you have several CLASS variables and you want to use reference coding for all of them, you can use PARAM=REF as an option on the class statement, as this program demonstrates. In this example, a UNITS statement is used so that the odds ratio for cholesterol is computed for each 10 units. ODS Graphics was turned on. Because there is no PLOTS= option, you will obtain a default plot that shows the odds ratios for each predictor in the model.

Only selected portions of the output are shown:

Class Level Information			
Class	Value	Design Variables	
Age_Group	1:< 60	0	0
	2:60-70	1	0
	3:71+	0	1
Gender	F	0	
	M	1	

Because Age_Group has three levels, SAS has created two dummy variables. Age_Group 1:< 60 is the reference group, so each of the dummy variables is equal to 0 for this age group.

Model Fit Statistics		
Criterion	Intercept Only	Intercept and Covariates
AIC	360.879	322.294
SC	365.093	343.367
-2 Log L	358.879	312.294

The fit has improved compared to the first two models, according to either the AIC or SC values.

Analysis of Maximum Likelihood Estimates						
Parameter		DF	Estimate	Standard Error	Wald Chi-Square	Pr > ChiSq
Intercept		1	-7.9956	1.2091	43.7300	<.0001
Gender	M	1	1.0028	0.3177	9.9632	0.0016
Age_Group	2:60-70	1	1.4050	0.5148	7.4487	0.0063
Age_Group	3:71+	1	1.9676	0.5092	14.9286	0.0001
Chol		1	0.0193	0.00505	14.5832	0.0001

All the predictors are significant.

Association of Predicted Probabilities and Observed Responses			
Percent Concordant	77.4	Somers' D	0.553
Percent Discordant	22.1	Gamma	0.555
Percent Tied	0.5	Tau-a	0.114
Pairs	25636	c	0.776

The concordance has improved and there are almost no ties.

Profile Likelihood Confidence Interval for Odds Ratios				
Effect	Unit	Estimate	95% Confidence Limits	
Gender M vs F	1.0000	2.726	1.486	5.198
Age_Group 2:60-70 vs 1:< 60	1.0000	4.076	1.601	12.547
Age_Group 3:71+ vs 1:< 60	1.0000	7.154	2.858	21.877
Chol	10.0000	1.213	1.101	1.343

The profile likelihood odds ratios are displayed in the output. The odds ratio for Gender is 2.726, slightly different from the value that resulted when Gender was the only predictor in the model. The reason for this outcome is that this odds ratio is adjusted for all the other predictors in the model. Subjects in the middle age group (60 to 70) have 4.076 times the odds of having a heart attack compared to the youngest age group; subjects in the oldest age group (71 and older) have 7.154 times the odds of having a heart attack compared to the youngest age group. Finally, the odds ratio for each 10 points of cholesterol is 1.213. Because none of the 95% confidence intervals includes 1, they are all significant at the .05 level. Because ODS Graphics was turned on for this program, you get the following plot:

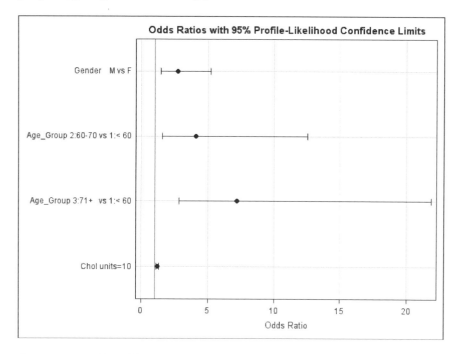

Here you see the odds ratios for each predictor variable, and the 95% CI.

Running a Logistic Regression with Interactions

When you use PROC LOGISTIC, you can specify main effects and interactions in your model. In this example, you enter the same three variables as in the previous model, along with all the possible two-way interactions. In addition, you use a backward elimination technique to build the model.

With the backward elimination method, main effects cannot be removed from the model if those effects are involved in an interaction that remains in the model. This kind of model is referred to in the literature as a hierarchical model.

With this program, you will also use ODS Graphics to produce plots of the odds ratios and an ROC curve.

An ROC curve shows the relationship between a false-positive rate and the sensitivity of the test. A false-positive rate is the proportion of time an observation without the outcome is predicted by the model to have the outcome (it is also equal to 1 minus the specificity). Sensitivity is the proportion of observations that have the outcome that is predicted by the model to have the outcome. Ideally, models have high sensitivity and low false-positive rates. You can change the sensitivity of your model (and, therefore, the false-positive rate) by choosing a lower probability as predictive of a positive outcome. An ROC curve gives you a visual representation of the relationship between the false-positive rate and the sensitivity.

As you might expect, this program will be a bit more complicated than any of the previous examples.

Program 11.5: Running a Logistic Model with Interactions

```
ods graphics on;
title "Running a Logistic Model with Interactions";
proc logistic data=risk plots(only)=(roc oddsratio);
   class Gender (param=ref ref='F')
         Age_Group (param=ref ref='1:< 60');
   model Heart_Attack (event = 'Yes') = Gender | Age_Group |
   Chol @2 /
         selection=backward slstay=.10 clodds=pl;
   units Chol=10;
   oddsratio Chol;
```

```
    oddsratio Gender;
    oddsratio Age_Group;
run;
quit;
ods graphics off;
```

This time, a PLOTS= option was added to request an ROC curve and a plot showing odds ratios. A short-cut notation was used in the MODEL statement to request a factorial model. This notation is the same notation you used with PROC GLM. As a review, the following two lines of code are equivalent:

```
model A | B | C;
```

```
model A B C A*B A*C B*C A*B*C;
```

To limit the model to interactions that are no higher than two-way interactions, you include @2 after the model specification.

Also in this program, the MODEL option SELECTION= was set to BACKWARD and the significance levels for staying in the model (SLSTAY) was set to .1 (in PROC LOGISTIC, the default value for SLSTAY in the backward selection method is .05). Three ODDSRATIO statements were also added. When you have interactions in a model, PROC LOGISTIC does not automatically compute odds ratios. The ODDSRATIO statement also has options that specify that you want odds ratios of one variable at a specified level of another variable. See the online *SAS/STAT User's Guide* for more information about the ODDSRATION statement.

Because the backward elimination method produces large volumes of output, only selected portions are shown:

Summary of Backward Elimination						
Step	Effect Removed		DF	Number In	Wald Chi-Square	Pr > ChiSq
1	Gender*Age_Group		2	5	4.0391	0.1327
2	Chol*Gender		1	4	0.8284	0.3627

Type 3 Analysis of Effects			
Effect	DF	Wald Chi-Square	Pr > ChiSq
Gender	1	9.9335	0.0016
Age_Group	2	10.5952	0.0050
Chol	1	6.2382	0.0125
Chol*Age_Group	2	8.9254	0.0115

This section of output shows that in Step 1, the Gender by Age_Group interaction was removed; in Step 2, the Chol by Gender interaction was removed. Because the p-values for all the remaining terms were less than .10 (the value of SLSTAY), no other terms were removed from the model. As mentioned previously, this is not always the case—if an interaction term is included in your model, each of the main effects involved in the interaction remain in the model, regardless of the p-value for these effects.

Model Fit Statistics		
Criterion	Intercept Only	Intercept and Covariates
AIC	360.879	315.635
SC	365.093	345.137
-2 Log L	358.879	301.635

This section of output shows the fit statistics for the final model. It is interesting to compare the AIC and SC values in this model with interactions to the model without interactions (Program 11.4).

Here is a summary of the AIC and SC value between the two models:

	Model without Interactions	Model with Interactions
AIC	322.294	315.635
SC	343.367	345.137

In the model that includes interactions, the AIC decreased (indicating a better model), but the SC value increased slightly. This seemingly contradictory result is explained by the fact that the SC value has a larger penalty for adding terms in the model. When you use the SC value to choose your best model, you often end up choosing the more parsimonious (simpler) model. In this example, adding interaction terms does little to improve the model, and you might decide to choose the simpler model.

Analysis of Maximum Likelihood Estimates						
Parameter		DF	Estimate	Standard Error	Wald Chi-Square	Pr > ChiSq
Intercept		1	-19.7757	6.7621	8.5525	0.0035
Gender	M	1	1.0044	0.3187	9.9335	0.0016
Age_Group	2:60-70	1	10.3576	7.0511	2.1577	0.1419
Age_Group	3:71+	1	16.3352	6.8787	5.6394	0.0176
Chol		1	0.0706	0.0283	6.2382	0.0125
Chol*Age_Group	2:60-70	1	-0.0383	0.0298	1.6599	0.1976
Chol*Age_Group	3:71+	1	-0.0639	0.0290	4.8579	0.0275

Here you see the parameter estimates for cholesterol, its interaction with age group, and the estimates and p-values for each of the dummy variables.

Association of Predicted Probabilities and Observed Responses			
Percent Concordant	78.7	Somers' D	0.577
Percent Discordant	21.0	Gamma	0.579
Percent Tied	0.4	Tau-a	0.119
Pairs	25636	c	0.788

The percent of concordant pairs is up to 78.7%, and there are almost no ties. The following table summarizes the predicted probabilities (and the c statistic) between the two models:

	Model without Interactions	**Model with Interactions**
Concordant Pairs	77.4	78.7
Discordant Pairs	22.1	21.1
Ties	.5	.1
c Statistic	.776	.788

All the measures for the model with interactions are improved, compared to the model without interactions. However, the improvements are small, and you might decide to choose the simpler model. The decision of which model to choose is often based on your knowledge of the data, as well as on the various fit statistics and measures of association.

Wald Confidence Interval for Odds Ratios		
Label	Estimate	95% Confidence Limits
Chol units=10 at Age_Group=1:< 60	2.027	1.164	3.529
Chol units=10 at Age_Group=2:60-70	1.382	1.153	1.656
Chol units=10 at Age_Group=3:71+	1.070	0.944	1.212
Gender F vs M	0.366	0.196	0.684
Age_Group 1:< 60 vs 2:60-70 at Chol=199.41	0.066	0.006	0.743
Age_Group 1:< 60 vs 3:71+ at Chol=199.41	0.028	0.003	0.300
Age_Group 2:60-70 vs 3:71+ at Chol=199.41	0.418	0.203	0.861

Profile Likelihood Confidence Interval for Odds Ratios			
Effect	Unit	Estimate	95% Confidence Limits
Gender M vs F	1.0000	2.730	1.485	5.212

Here you see the odds ratios for main effects and odds ratios for variables involved in the interaction. The value of cholesterol in this section of the output (199.41) is the mean cholesterol value.

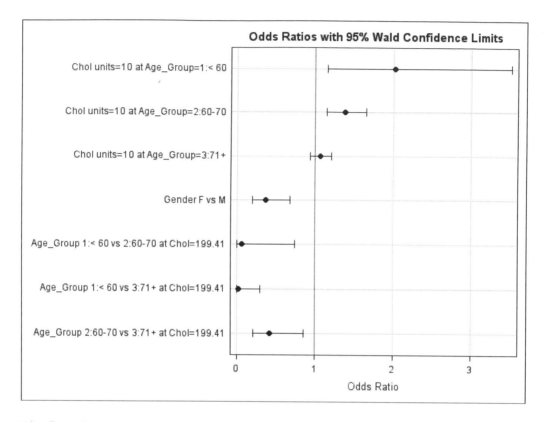

The first plot produced by ODS Graphics shows information about the odds ratios for the main effects, as well as those involved in interactions.

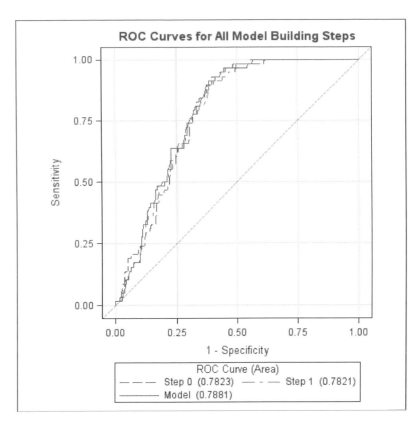

Two ROC plots are produced. One shows only the final model ROC. The one displayed here shows the ROC curve at each step of the backward elimination process. Based on the earlier discussion of ROC curves, the more area under the curve (which is the case with models that have a higher sensitivity for a given false-positive value), the more ideal the model. In this example, there is almost no difference between the ROC curves in the three steps.

Conclusions

In this chapter, you learned how you can use logistic regression to predict dichotomous outcomes. You can extend logistic regression to predict multinomial and ordinal outcomes.

You learned how you can use combinations of categorical and continuous variables as predictor variables. Just as with PROC REG, PROC LOGISTIC enables you to specify a model or to use one of several selection methods for building your model.

The next chapter covers a variety of nonparametric techniques. These techniques are particularly useful when you have small samples or when you are not completely satisfied that the assumptions for parametric tests are satisfied.

Nonparametric Tests

Introduction

SAS provides several nonparametric tests, such as the Wilcoxon rank-sum test, the Wilcoxon signed-rank test, and a Kruskal-Wallis analysis of variance. This chapter describes these tests, as well as a way to convert your data values to ranks, so that you can then run parametric tests on the ranked data.

Performing a Wilcoxon Rank-Sum Test

As an example, suppose you want to test whether incomes in the `Salary` data set are equal for men and women. You might first want to look at a histogram and probability plot of this variable for each value of Gender. You can use PROC UNIVARIATE to do this:

Program 12.1: Plotting the Distribution of Income

```
title "Displaying the Distribution of Incomes in the Salary Data Set";
proc univariate data=salary;
    id Subj;
    class Gender;
    var Income;
    histogram / normal;
    probplot / normal(mu=est sigma=est);
run;
```

Here are the two plots:

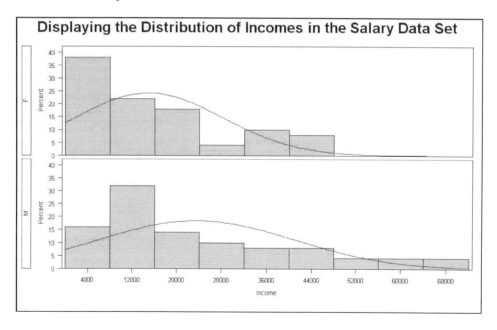

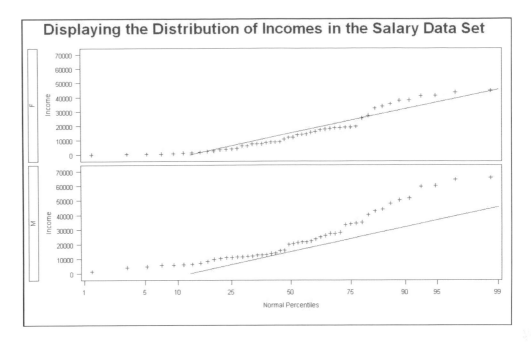

Displaying the Distribution of Incomes in the Salary Data Set

After looking at these two plots, you decide that a *t*-test is not appropriate with distributions that are so positively skewed. You decide to use a Wilcoxon rank-sum test (equivalent to the Mann-Whitney U test), to compare incomes by gender. (An alternative would be to look for a transformation such as a log transform that would make the distribution closer to normal.) The following program demonstrates how to perform this test:

Program 12.2: Performing a Wilcoxon Rank-Sum Test (aka Mann-Whitney U Test)

```
title "Performing a Wilcoxon Rank Sum Test";
proc npar1way data=Salary wilcoxon;
   class Gender;
   var Income;
run;
```

PROC NPAR1WAY runs a variety of nonparametric tests. The option WILCOXON is a request to run the Wilcoxon rank-sum test. The remaining statements look identical to those used with PROC TTEST. You specify the independent variable with a CLASS statement and one or more dependent variables with a VAR statement. Here is the result:

Performing a Wilcoxon Rank Sum Test

The NPAR1WAY Procedure

Wilcoxon Scores (Rank Sums) for Variable Income Classified by Variable Gender					
Gender	N	Sum of Scores	Expected Under H0	Std Dev Under H0	Mean Score
M	50	2927.0	2525.0	145.057460	58.540
F	50	2123.0	2525.0	145.057460	42.460

Wilcoxon Two-Sample Test	
Statistic	2927.0000
Normal Approximation	
Z	2.7679
One-Sided Pr > Z	0.0028
Two-Sided Pr > |Z|	0.0056
t Approximation	
One-Sided Pr > Z	0.0034
Two-Sided Pr > |Z|	0.0067
Z includes a continuity correction of 0.5.	

Kruskal-Wallis Test	
Chi-Square	7.6802
DF	1
Pr > Chi-Square	0.0056

With an *n* of 50 in each group, you can probably choose to use the normal approximation result, where you see a p-value of .0056. If you have small sample sizes, you might choose to include an EXACT statement in the procedure. An EXACT statement causes an exact p-value to be calculated. Do not use this statement if you have large sample sizes, because the processing time can become excessive, which will cause your CPU to overheat, your computer to catch fire, and you to lose your job (just kidding). Using an EXACT statement with this data set yielded a p-value of .0053, which is very close to the normal approximation value. The following program shows a modification of Program 12.2 and requests an exact p-value:

Program 12.3: Requesting an Exact p-Value for a Wilcoxon Rank-Sum Test

```
title "Performing a Wilcoxon Rank Sum Test";
title2 "Requesting an Exact p-Value";
proc nparlway data=Salary wilcoxon;
    class Gender;
    var Income;
    exact;
run;
```

Performing a Wilcoxon Signed-Rank Test (for Paired Data)

There is no direct way to run a nonparametric paired comparison—you first need to compute a variable that represents the difference of the two paired values, using a DATA step. You can then use PROC UNIVARIATE to perform the Wilcoxon signed-rank test.

As an example, you can use the `reading` data set, which contains a subject number (Subj), and before (variable Before) and after (variable After) reading speed scores. Here is a program that creates the difference variable and runs the analysis:

Program 12.4: Performing a Wilcoxon Signed-Rank Test

```
data difference;
    set reading;
    Diff = After - Before;
run;

ods select testsforlocation;
title "Performing a Wilcoxon Signed Rank Test";
proc univariate data=difference;
    var Diff;
run;
```

The short DATA step creates the difference variable (Diff). Because PROC UNIVARIATE creates so much output, this program uses an ODS SELECT statement to restrict the output to the section called Tests For Location. This statement is strictly optional—if you omit it, you get the complete output listing from this procedure.

Here is the output:

Performing a Wilcoxon Signed Rank Test

The UNIVARIATE Procedure
Variable: Diff

Tests for Location: Mu0=0				
Test		Statistic	p Value	
Student's t	t	3.019386	Pr > |t|	0.0194
Sign	M	3	Pr >= |M|	0.0703
Signed Rank	S	16.5	Pr >= |S|	0.0234

You see three tests: one is a parametric test, and the other two are nonparametric tests of location. The sign test computes the probability that there are more observations that are greater than or less than zero than would be expected under the null hypothesis. The p-value .0703 reflects this test's low power. The last line of the output shows you the results of the Wilcoxon signed-rank test. Here the result is significant (p = .0234). In this example, you could have used a *t*-test, but it was convenient to use a nonparametric paired comparison for this data set. Looking at the output, you can see that the p-value, using a *t*-test (.0194), is not that much different from the p-value that was obtained by using a nonparametric test.

Performing a Kruskal-Wallis One-Way ANOVA

If the normality assumptions for a one-way analysis of variance (ANOVA) are not met, you might want to run the nonparametric equivalent test known as the Kruskal-Wallis ANOVA. The same statements that you used to run the Wilcoxon rank-sum test also run a Kruskal-Wallis ANOVA when your class variable has more than two levels.

To demonstrate this, you can use the `store` data set that contains, among other variables, a region of the country (Region) and the amount of money spent on music (Music_Sales). Here is the code:

Program 12.5: Performing a Kruskal-Wallis ANOVA

```
title "Performing a Kruskal-Wallis ANOVA";
proc nparlway data=store wilcoxon;
   class Region;
   var Music_Sales;
run;
```

As with the Wilcoxon rank-sum test, you can include an EXACT statement in this procedure if you have a small sample size and do not want to use normal approximations. Here is the output:

Performing a Kruskal-Wallis ANOVA

The NPAR1WAY Procedure

Wilcoxon Scores (Rank Sums) for Variable Music_Sales Classified by Variable Region					
Region	N	Sum of Scores	Expected Under H0	Std Dev Under H0	Mean Score
West	50	3232.00	5025.00	352.792165	64.640000
South	45	4426.00	4522.50	340.220443	98.355556
North	69	7503.50	6934.50	387.300888	108.746377
East	36	4938.50	3618.00	313.012351	137.180556
Average scores were used for ties.					

Kruskal-Wallis Test	
Chi-Square	35.4423
DF	3
Pr > Chi-Square	<.0001

The result (p<.0001) indicates that music sales medians were not equal among the four regions of the country.

Comparing Spread: The Ansari-Bradley Test

The Ansari-Bradley test is a nonparametric alternative to the folded F-test for comparing variances. To demonstrate this test, the following program presents a short DATA step, which creates two groups of scores, followed by the Ansari-Bradley test.

Program 12.6: Performing the Ansari-Bradley Test for Spread

```
data twogroups;
   do Group = 'One','Two';
      do Subj = 1 to 15;
         input Score @;
         output;
      end;
   end;
datalines;
1 3 5 7 11 20 25 30 40 55 66 77 88 90 100
2 4 8 20 24 33 40 45 55 59 60 68 69 70 71
;
title "Performing the Ansari-Bradley Test for Spread";
proc npar1way data=twogroups ab;
   class Group;
   var Score;
run;
```

This DATA step creates a data set with three variables: Group, Subj, and Score. All the values in the first line of data belong to Group One and all the values in the second line of data belong to Group Two.

Let's look at how this DATA step works in more detail. (If you are interested only in how to run statistical tests, and you do not need the details of this DATA step, feel free to skip this paragraph.) The outer DO loop first sets the value for Group equal to One. It is quite convenient that you can use SAS DO loops to loop through character values as well as numeric values. The inner DO loop creates Subj values from 1 to 15. Inside this loop, you read in the 15 Score values. The single at sign (@) on the INPUT statement is an instruction to hold the line. You need this because each time SAS executes an INPUT statement in a DATA step, it wants to read data from a new line. The @ (called a single trailing at sign, by the way) prevents SAS from going to a new line when it executes more than one INPUT statement in a DATA step. Following the INPUT statement is an OUTPUT statement that causes an observation to be written to the resulting data set. After the first 15 observations with Group='One' have been written out, the outer DO loop sets the value of Group to Two and the next 15 observations are created.

The AB option on PROC NPAR1WAY requests the Ansari-Bradley test. As with the previous examples that used PROC NPAR1WAY, you have the option of including an EXACT statement when you have small samples and you do not want to use a normal approximation to compute the p-value. PROC NPAR1WAY gives you the following output:

Performing the Ansari-Bradley Test for Spread

The NPAR1WAY Procedure

Ansari-Bradley Scores for Variable Score Classified by Variable Group					
Group	N	Sum of Scores	Expected Under H0	Std Dev Under H0	Mean Score
One	15	104.0	120.0	12.023684	6.933333
Two	15	136.0	120.0	12.023684	9.066667
Average scores were used for ties.					

Ansari-Bradley Two-Sample Test	
Statistic	104.0000
Z	-1.3307
One-Sided Pr < Z	0.0916
Two-Sided Pr > |Z|	0.1833

Ansari-Bradley One-Way Analysis	
Chi-Square	1.7708
DF	1
Pr > Chi-Square	0.1833

The Ansari-Bradley test for scale differences can be used when you have two groups or more than two groups. In this example, because you are comparing distributions between two groups, the results from the two-sample test and the one-way analysis are equivalent. In both cases, you fail to reject the null hypothesis of equal dispersion (or scale differences) between the two groups (with alpha=.05).

Converting Data Values into Ranks

When you have data values that are not normally distributed, one option is to replace the data values with ranks, and then perform parametric tests on the ranks. PROC RANK takes a SAS data set as input and creates another data set as output, in which data values are converted to ranks. To fully understand how PROC RANK works, take a moment to review the following example:

Program 12.7: Demonstrating PROC RANK

```
data one;
   input Subj x y;
datalines;
1 3 100
2 1 200
3 5 300
4 77 400
;
proc rank data=one out=two;
   var x;
   ranks Rank_x;
run;

title "Listing of data set TWO";
proc print data=two noobs;
run;
```

You specify your input data set on the DATA= option and your output data set on the OUT= option. Here is the listing of data set TWO:

Listing of data set TWO

Subj	x	y	Rank_x
1	3	100	2
2	1	200	1
3	5	300	3
4	77	400	4

You will notice several interesting things about the data set that PROC RANK creates. First, all of the variables from the input data set appear in the output data set, even if they are not listed in the VAR statement. Next, you list all of the variables for which you want to compute ranks on the VAR statement. If you do not include a RANKS statement, the values of the variables listed on the VAR statement are *replaced* with their ranks. Therefore, it is a good idea to always include a list of new variable names on a RANKS statement. Each variable that is listed on this RANKS statement contains the ranks of each variable on the VAR statement. You are free to choose any names you want for these new variables.

As an example that shows how to use PROC RANK, the next program converts the Income values from the `salary` data set (these values were positively skewed) into ranks. These ranks are then used to perform a two-sample *t*-test. The program is intended to demonstrate how to use PROC RANK in combination with procedures that perform parametric tests. Here is the program:

Program 12.8: Replacing Values with Ranks and Running a *t*-Test

```
proc rank data=salary out=rank_salary;
    var Income;
    ranks Rank_of_Salary;
run;

title "Converting Data to Ranks and Performing a T-Test";
proc ttest data=rank_salary;
    class Gender;
    var Rank_of_Salary;
run;
```

A portion of the output looks like this:

Converting Data to Ranks and Performing a T-Test

The TTEST Procedure

Variable: Rank_of_Salary (Rank for Variable Income)

Method	Variances	DF	t Value	Pr > |t|
Pooled	Equal	98	-2.87	0.0050
Satterthwaite	Unequal	97.531	-2.87	0.0050

Equality of Variances				
Method	Num DF	Den DF	F Value	Pr > F
Folded F	49	49	1.15	0.6288

If you choose to use the assumption of equal variance (which seems reasonable here), you see a p-value of .0050. This is very close to the p-value that you obtained from the Wilcoxon rank-sum test at the beginning of this chapter (p=.0056 using a normal approximation and p=.0053 using the EXACT statement).

Using PROC RANK to Group Your Data Values

Although this discussion is slightly off topic for this chapter, it is related to PROC RANK. Because you have learned how to use PROC RANK to convert raw data values into ranks, this seems a good opportunity to demonstrate another very useful feature of PROC RANK—the ability to create ordered groups from your data.

The PROC RANK option GROUPS=n divides your data values into n groups. Somewhat counter intuitively, the n groups are numbered from 0 to n–1. To see how this works, Program 12.9 creates a new variable called Salary_Group from the Income data. Because you specify GROUPS=4, the Salary_Group variable has the values 0 to 3. Here is the program:

Program 12.9: Using PROC RANK to Create Groups

```
title "Using PROC RANK to Create Groups";
proc rank data=salary out=new_salary groups=4;
   var Income;
   ranks Salary_Group;
run;
proc print data=new_salary(obs=10) noobs;
run;
```

The first 10 observations from the data set `new_salary` look like this:

Using PROC RANK to Create Groups

Subj	Gender	Income	Salary_Group
1	M	27265	2
1	F	17152	2
2	M	20347	2
2	F	3636	0
3	M	64347	3
3	F	41292	3
4	M	27961	3
4	F	2556	0
5	M	4114	0
5	F	8554	1

Your new variable, Salary_Group takes the values 0 to 3.

Conclusions

Hopefully, this chapter has demonstrated that it is quite easy to run nonparametric statistics using SAS. When you have doubts about whether the assumptions for a parametric test have been met, try out one of the nonparametric routines demonstrated in this chapter. It is often instructive to perform both a parametric and a nonparametric test on your data, and see if you come to similar conclusions.

The next chapter covers how to use SAS to compute power and sample size.

Power and Sample Size

Introduction

SAS has extensive programs for determining power and sample size for a wide variety of designs. You have a choice: you can run PROC POWER (or GLMPOWER for more advanced GLM designs) and make your requests using appropriate statements or you can choose to run an interactive program called SAS Power and Sample Size that allows you to use a menu system to perform your calculations. The SAS Power and Sample Size program is included with SAS/STAT software.

Whether you decide to use the SAS procedures or to run the interactive program, you can specify your design (two-sample *t*-test, ANOVA, comparing proportions, etc.) and then let the program compute either the power or sample size. Whichever method you choose, you can specify multiple scenarios for various parameters, such as a family of mean differences or a choice of several standard deviations. You can also request output in graphical form. For example, you can plot sample size against power for a family of theoretical values for your parameters.

This chapter starts by demonstrating how to use PROC POWER to compute the power or sample size for some simple designs: a two-sample *t*-test, a one-way ANOVA, and the difference of two proportions. The remainder of the chapter will demonstrate how to run the interactive Power and Sample Size application.

Computing the Sample Size for an Unpaired *t*-Test

Let's start with an example that computes the number of subjects per group for several scenarios. Two pairs of means, 20.0 versus 30.0 and 22.0 versus 28.0, are hypothesized. You want to see sample sizes for grouped standard deviations of 10 and 15. Next, you want to see the sample sizes for powers of 80% and 90%. These combinations yield 2x2x2=8 combinations. Finally, you want to see a plot of power versus the number of subjects per group for all eight combinations. Here is the program:

Program 13.1: Computing Sample Size for an Unpaired *t*-Test

```
title "Sample Size Requirements for a T-Test";
proc power;
   twosamplemeans
   groupmeans = (20 30) (22 28)
   stddev = 10 15
   power= .80 .90
   npergroup = .;
   plot x = power min = .70 max = .90;
run;
```

You specify that you want calculations for a two sample *t*-test by using the keyword TWOSAMPLEMEANS. The two pairs of means that you want are placed in parentheses after the keyword GROUPMEANS=. In this program, one test will be conducted with a mean of 20 versus 30 and another with a mean of 22 versus 28. You specify standard deviation with the STDDEV= keyword and list the two standard deviations of interest. Next, you list .80 and .90 after the keyword POWER. (Note that power is expressed as a proportion and not as a percentage.) The procedure can compute either power or sample size (or other parameters if you want to). You specify the parameter you want to compute by entering a missing value for that parameter. In this example, you entered a missing value for NPERGROUP, so that is what will be calculated. Finally, a PLOT statement indicates that you want to plot power on the x-axis with powers that range from .70 to .90. Because you did not enter a value for alpha, it defaults to alpha=.05.

Here is the output:

Sample Size Requirements for a T-Test

The POWER Procedure
Two-sample t Test for Mean Difference

Fixed Scenario Elements	
Distribution	Normal
Method	Exact
Number of Sides	2
Null Difference	0
Alpha	0.05

Computed N Per Group						
Index	Mean1	Mean2	Std Dev	Nominal Power	Actual Power	N Per Group
1	20	30	10	0.8	0.807	17
2	20	30	10	0.9	0.912	23
3	20	30	15	0.8	0.808	37
4	20	30	15	0.9	0.904	49
5	22	28	10	0.8	0.804	45
6	22	28	10	0.9	0.903	60
7	22	28	15	0.8	0.804	100
8	22	28	15	0.9	0.901	133

Here you see the sample size per group that is needed to achieve powers of 80% or 90% for each combination of hypothesized means and standard deviations. For example, if your two means were 20 and 30 and you estimated the pooled standard deviation to be 10, the actual power of your study would be .807. Because the number of subjects per group must be an integer (it is rounded up when a power calculation is conducted), the actual power might be slightly higher than the power that is used in the calculations.

The PLOT request produced the following output:

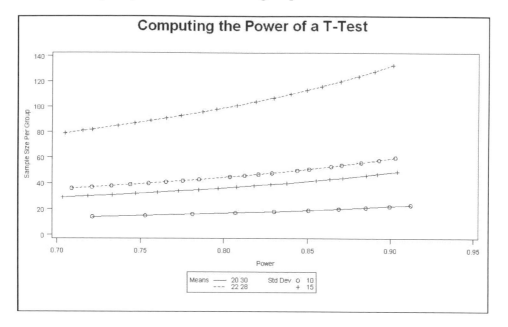

This plot shows the sample size versus power for each combination of hypothesized mean differences and standard deviation.

Computing the Power of an Unpaired *t*-Test

This example is similar to the previous example, except that you now want to compute power for a given sample size. In this example, you think that one group (the control) will have a mean close to 20. You want to compute power for the case in which the second group has a mean of 30 or 35. You also want to see the effect of a standard deviation equal to 10 or 15. Finally, you want to compute power for sample sizes of 30 and 35 per group. Here is the program:

Program 13.2: Computing the Power of a *t*-Test

```
title "Computing the Power of a T-Test";
proc power;
   twosamplemeans
   groupmeans = 20 | 30 35
   stddev = 10 15
   power= .
   npergroup = 30 35;
   plot x = n min = 20 max = 50;
run;
```

A different notation was used on the GROUPMEANS= parameter. The vertical bar indicates a crossing—every value on one side of the bar versus every value on the other side of the bar. In this program, you want to compare a mean of 20 versus 30 and a mean of 20 versus 35. As in Program 13.1, you specify multiple values for the standard deviation. The POWER value is set to missing, which means that this procedure will compute power for the given sample sizes. The PLOT request places *n* per group on the x-axis, with *n* ranging from 20 to 50. Here is the output:

Computing the Power of a T-Test

The POWER Procedure
Two-sample t Test for Mean Difference

Fixed Scenario Elements	
Distribution	Normal
Method	Exact
Group 1 Mean	20
Number of Sides	2
Null Difference	0
Alpha	0.05

Computed Power			
Index	Mean2	Std Dev	N Per Group	Power
1	30	10	30	0.968
2	30	10	35	0.985
3	30	15	30	0.719
4	30	15	35	0.785
5	35	10	30	>.999
6	35	10	35	>.999
7	35	15	30	0.968
8	35	15	35	0.985

This table is similar to the one in the previous example, except that you now see the resulting power for combinations of means, standard deviations, and the number of subjects per group.

The following output shows the PLOT result:

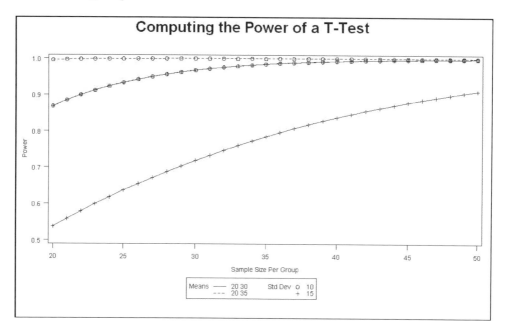

Computing Sample Size for an ANOVA Design

If you want to compute the sample size for an ANOVA design (or compute power, given a sample size), you can use PROC POWER with the keyword ONEWAYANOVA. For more complex ANOVA designs, you can use PROC GLMPOWER (this procedure is not covered in this chapter, but it is included in the *SAS/STAT User's Guide*).

In this example, you want to determine the sample size that you need for a one-way ANOVA design with three groups. You hypothesize that the means for each of three groups are 20, 25, and 30. You want to see the effect of two standard deviations (8 and 10) for powers of 80% and 90%. Here is the program:

Program 13.3: Computing the Power for an ANOVA Design

```
title "Computing the Power for an ANOVA Model";
proc power;
   onewayanova
   groupmeans = 20 | 25 | 30
   stddev = 8 10
   power = .80 .90
   npergroup = .;
   plot x = power min = .70 max = .90;
run;
```

Because you want to compute the sample size per group, you set NPERGROUP equal to a missing value. Additional options for computing power for ANOVA designs let you analyze unbalanced designs.

The following tabular output and the plots are produced by this program:

Computing the Power for an ANOVA Model

The POWER Procedure
Overall F Test for One-Way ANOVA

Fixed Scenario Elements	
Method	Exact
Group Means	20 25 30
Alpha	0.05

Computed N Per Group				
Index	Std Dev	Nominal Power	Actual Power	N Per Group
1	8	0.8	0.820	14
2	8	0.9	0.913	18
3	10	0.8	0.815	21
4	10	0.9	0.908	27

For each combination of hypothesized standard deviations, you see the number of subjects per group that is needed to achieve powers of 80% and 90%.

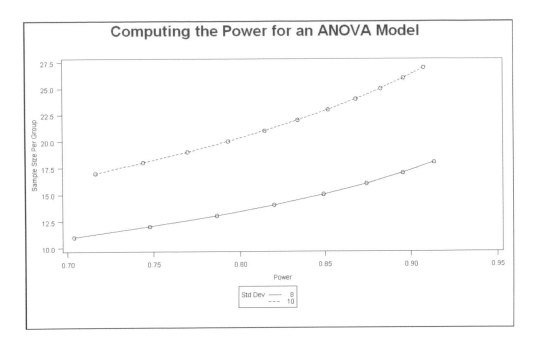

Here you see the sample size per group that is needed versus power for standard deviations of 8 and 10.

Computing Sample Sizes (or Power) for a Difference in Two Proportions

In this example, you want to know how many subjects you need in each group to compare a base-line proportion of .15 against three possible values: .20, .225, and .25. You want to do this for powers of .80 and .90. Here is the program:

Program 13.4: Computing Sample Size for a Difference in Two Proportions

```
title "Computing Sample Size for a Difference in Two Proportions";
proc power;
   twosamplefreq
   test = pchi
   groupproportions = .15 | .20 .225 .25
   power = .80 .90
   npergroup = .;
   plot x = power min = .70 max = .90;
run;
```

In this example, the test statistic is Pearson's chi-square. Other choices are Fisher's exact test (TEST=FISHER) or likelihood ratio chi-square test (TEST=LRCHI). The vertical bar (crossing operator) indicates that you want to compare the base rate of .15 against the three values listed after the bar. Two powers are specified (.80 and .90), and the NPERGROUP is set to a missing value. Power calculations for two proportions are very flexible: you can specify different numbers of subjects per group, compute power or sample size based on a specified odds ratio, and so forth. See the *SAS/STAT User's Guide*.

The following tabular and graphical outputs result from this procedure:

Computing Sample Size for a Difference in Two Proportions

The POWER Procedure
Pearson Chi-square Test for Two Proportions

Fixed Scenario Elements	
Distribution	Asymptotic normal
Method	Normal approximation
Group 1 Proportion	0.15
Number of Sides	2
Null Proportion Difference	0
Alpha	0.05

Computed N Per Group				
Index	Proportion2	Nominal Power	Actual Power	N Per Group
1	0.200	0.8	0.800	906
2	0.200	0.9	0.900	1212
3	0.225	0.8	0.800	424
4	0.225	0.9	0.900	568
5	0.250	0.8	0.800	250
6	0.250	0.9	0.901	335

Notice that the number of subjects per group can be quite large when you want to show small differences in proportions and you also require high power.

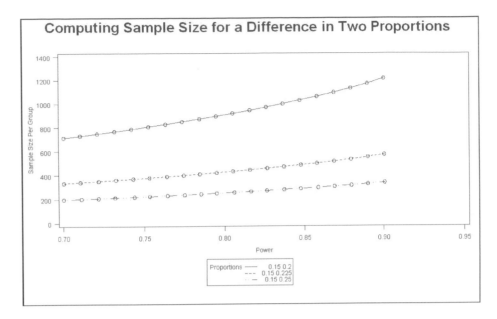

This plot also demonstrates the large sample sizes that are required to show small differences in proportions when you also require high power.

Using the SAS Power and Sample Size Interactive Application

This section shows how to run the interactive Power and Sample Size application. You can send this program to your desktop as an icon if you plan to use it frequently.

You start by clicking the Microsoft Start button and proceed as follows:

Start→All Programs→SAS→SAS Power and Sample Size

Because this application is menu driven, you can pretty much figure things out for yourself. To help you get started, let's redo the unpaired *t*-test power calculation that started this chapter.

After the SAS Power and Sample Size application starts, click File→New. You will see the following window:

Because you want to compute sample size for a two-sample *t*-test, select that option. The following window opens:

If you want to compute sample size, you can select either of the last two buttons. This example uses Sample size per group.

Now you select the appropriate tabs to enter your choices of means, standard deviations, and power (or sample size if you want the program to compute power). The next window demonstrates how you can enter means:

The windows in which you enter the standard deviations and power are not shown because they are very straightforward. This demonstration uses two values for standard deviation (10 and 15) and two powers (.8 and .9).

The next two screen captures show the tabular output and the power versus sample size plots. (Note that the CUSTOM button was used on the graph, with Sample Size selected for the vertical axis.)

```
              Two-sample t Test for Mean Difference

                    Fixed Scenario Elements

              Distribution              Normal
              Method                    Exact
              Number of Sides              2
              Alpha                     0.05
              Null Difference              0


                    Computed N Per Group

                              Std    Nominal    Actual    N Per
        Index   Mean1   Mean2  Dev    Power      Power     Group

          1      20      30    10      0.8       0.807      17
          2      20      30    10      0.9       0.912      23
          3      20      30    15      0.8       0.808      37
          4      20      30    15      0.9       0.904      49
          5      22      28    10      0.8       0.804      45
          6      22      28    10      0.9       0.903      60
          7      22      28    15      0.8       0.804     100
          8      22      20    15      0.9       0.901     133
```

This listing is identical to the output from Program 13.1. Although this author does not usually prefer point-and-click applications over "real" programming, this is one instance in which the interactive application works very well.

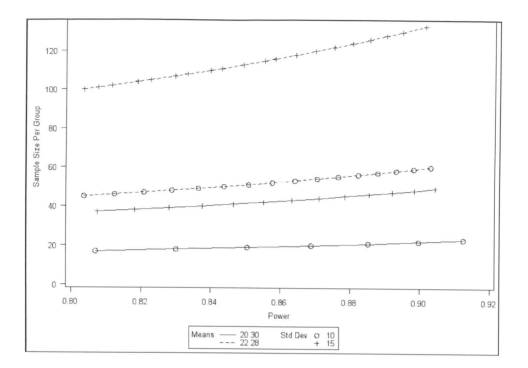

Conclusions

Whether you write your own program using PROC POWER (or PROC GLMPOWER) or use the SAS Power and Sample Size interactive program, you can quickly and easily compute power and sample size for many different statistical tests.

As a personal note, during my 26 years as a researcher at the Robert Wood Johnson Medical School, the most common questions I was asked involved power and sample size. This was before SAS had developed its power and sample size programs. The ability to examine the relationship between power and sample size for several hypothesized scenarios and to see the results in graphical and tabular form would have been invaluable.

The next, and last, chapter in this book describes how to select random samples from SAS data sets.

Selecting Random Samples

Introduction

SAS/STAT software includes a procedure called SURVEYSELECT that you can use to select random samples from a SAS data set. You have a choice of a simple random sample (without replacement), an unrestricted random sample (with replacement), or more complicated samples that include stratification or probability-proportional-to-size (PPS) sampling. This chapter demonstrates how to select random samples with and without replacement. For details on more complicated schema, see the *SAS/STAT User's Guide* (available on your SAS Help menu).

Taking a Simple Random Sample

PROC SURVEYSELECT lets you take a simple random sample from a SAS data set by specifying the sample size or by specifying the proportion of the input data set that you want to select. You also have control over how SAS chooses the seed value that it uses to create the random sequence. If you supply a fixed seed, then each time you run the procedure you obtain the same sample. A fixed seed is useful if you need to create the exact same random sample at another time. If you do not supply a seed, you obtain a different random sample each time you run the procedure.

In the example that follows, you want to take a 10% random sample from the `risk` data set (which contains 500 observations), and you want to supply a fixed seed:

Program 14.1: Taking a Simple Random Sample

```
title "Taking a Simple Random Sample";
proc surveyselect data=risk out=risk_sample
   method = srs
   samprate = .1
   seed = 1357924;
run;
```

You identify the input data set with DATA= and the output data set with OUT=. METHOD=SRS indicates that you want a simple random sample. This sampling method ensures that each observation in your input data set has an equal probability of being selected and that the same observation cannot be selected more than once (selection without replacement). To specify a 10% sample, you set the option SAMPRATE equal to .1. To specify a sample size rather than a sampling rate, use the SAMPSIZE= option instead. To specify a seed value, use the SEED= option and select any integer for this value (larger numbers, 7 to 9 digits in length, are preferred).

Here is the output from this program:

Taking a Simple Random Sample

The SURVEYSELECT Procedure

Selection Method	Simple Random Sampling

Input Data Set	RISK
Random Number Seed	1357924
Sampling Rate	0.1
Sample Size	50
Selection Probability	0.1
Sampling Weight	10
Output Data Set	RISK_SAMPLE

Taking a Random Sample with Replacement

To demonstrate how to select a random sample with replacement, let's use the reading data set and create a sample of size 5. This data set has only eight observations so there is a high likelihood of selecting an observation from the input data set more than once. Here is the program:

Program 14.2: Taking a Random Sample with Replacement

```
title "Taking a Random Sample with Replacement";
proc surveyselect data=reading out=read_replace
   outhits
   method = urs
   sampsize = 5
   seed = 1324354;
run;

title "Listing of Data Set READ_REPLACE";
proc print data=read_replace;
run;
```

The method URS (unrestricted random sampling) is a sampling method that allows an observation from the input data set to be selected more than once. An option called OUTHITS was included in this program. Without this option, any observation that is selected more than once produces only a single observation in the output data set. You can tell that an observation was selected more than once by looking at the variable NumberHits. This variable is added to the output data set by the procedure and it tells you how many times an observation from the input data set was selected. When you use the OUTHITS option, you still get the NumberHits variable, but the output data set now contains multiple observations for an observation that was selected multiple times.

Here is the output from PROC SURVEYSELECT and a listing of the resulting data set:

Taking a Random Sample with Replacement

The SURVEYSELECT Procedure

Selection Method	Unrestricted Random Sampling

Input Data Set	READING
Random Number Seed	1324354
Sample Size	5
Expected Number of Hits	0.625
Sampling Weight	1.6
Output Data Set	READ_REPLACE

Listing of Data Set READ_REPLACE

Obs	Subj	Before	After	NumberHits
1	1	100	110	1
2	6	133	137	1
3	7	210	209	1
4	8	155	179	2
5	8	155	179	2

The last two observations in this data set (Subj=8) resulted from the OUTHITS option.

To help you understand how the OUTHITS options affects your random sample, let's run Program 14.2 again, but with this option removed.

Program 14.3: Rerunning the Program without the OUTHITS Option

```
title "Taking a Random Sample with Replacement";
title2 "Omitting the OUTHITS Option";
proc surveyselect data=reading out=read_replace
   method = urs
   sampsize = 5
   seed = 1324354;
run;

title "Listing of Data Set READ_REPLACE - OUTHITS Option Removed";
proc print data=read_replace;
run;
```

Here is the output:

Taking a Random Sample with Replacement
Omitting the OUTHITS Option

The SURVEYSELECT Procedure

Selection Method	Unrestricted Random Sampling

Input Data Set	READING
Random Number Seed	1324354
Sample Size	5
Expected Number of Hits	0.625
Sampling Weight	1.6
Output Data Set	READ_REPLACE

Listing of Data Set READ_REPLACE - OUTHITS Option Removed

Obs	Subj	Before	After	NumberHits
1	1	100	110	1
2	6	133	137	1
3	7	210	209	1
4	8	155	179	2

Notice that now you have four observations (Subj=8 has one observation); the variable NumberHits tells you that subject 8 was selected twice.

Creating Replicate Samples using PROC SURVEYSELECT

You can include a REPS= option with PROC SURVEYSELECT to create a data set that includes replicates of your sample. This choice can be useful for bootstrap methods and some Monte Carlo techniques.

To see how this works, the following program creates three replicate random samples of size 5 from the `risk` data set.

Program 14.4: Requesting Replicate Samples

```
title "Requesting Replicate Samples";
proc surveyselect data=risk out=riskrep
   method = srs
   sampsize = 5
   reps = 3
   seed = 1357924;
run;

title "Listing of Data Set RISKREP";
proc print data=riskrep;
run;
```

This example uses the SAMPSIZE option instead of the SAMPRATE option that was used in Program 14.1. The REPS=3 option creates three replicate random samples. When you use the REPS= option, the resulting data set contains a variable called Replicate that identifies which replicate a particular observation belongs to. Here is a listing of that data set:

Listing of Data Set RISKREP

Obs	Replicate	Age_Group	Gender	Age	Chol	Heart_Attack
1	1	3:71+	F	80	178	No
2	1	2:60-70	M	69	256	No
3	1	1:< 60	M	58	229	No
4	1	3:71+	F	71	171	No
5	1	2:60-70	F	69	207	No
6	2	3:71+	M	74	233	No
7	2	1:< 60	F	56	191	No
8	2	3:71+	M	72	198	No
9	2	3:71+	M	79	165	No
10	2	3:71+	F	77	150	No
11	3	2:60-70	M	62	271	No
12	3	2:60-70	M	69	203	No
13	3	2:60-70	F	66	220	No
14	3	2:60-70	F	62	204	No
15	3	2:60-70	F	66	183	No

This listing shows that there are three replicates of five observations each.

Conclusions

Although you can use DATA step programming to create random samples, PROC SURVEYSELECT is easier, and in many cases, more efficient than the alternatives. See the SAS OnlineDoc if you require samples based on a more complicated schema.

References

Allison, Paul D. 1999. *Logistic Regression Using SAS: Theory and Application*. Cary, NC: SAS Institute Inc.

Cody, Ronald P. and Jeffrey K. Smith. 2005. *Applied Statistics and the SAS Programming Language, Fifth Edition*. Englewood Cliffs, NJ: Prentice Hall

SAS Institute Inc. "Statistical Graphics with ODS Course Notes." ISBN 978-1-60764-334-0. Cary, NC: SAS Institute Inc.

SAS Institute Inc. "Statistics 1: Introduction to ANOVA, Regression, and Logistic Regression Course Notes." ISBN 978-1-59994-914-7. Cary, NC: SAS Institute Inc.

Index